# Empowering Words

# Empowering Words
## Extracts from the Letters and Messages of Shoghi Effendi for Inspiration, Guidance and Vision

Copyright 2012, Juxta Publishing Limited.

ISBN 978-0-9698024-5-7

*This book has been produced with the consent of the original authors or rights holders. Authors or rights holders retain full rights to their works. Requests to reproduce the contents of this work can be directed to the individual authors or rights holders directly or to Juxta Publishing Limited. Reproduction of this book in its current form is governed by the Juxta Publishing Books for the World license outlined below.*

This book is released as part of Juxta Publishing's Books for the World program which aims to provide the widest possible access to quality Bahá'í-inspired literature to readers around the world. Use of this book is governed by the Juxta Publishing Books for the World license:

1. This book is available in printed and electronic forms.

2. This book may be freely redistributed in electronic form so long as the following conditions are met:

    a. The contents of the file are not altered
    b. This copyright notice remains intact
    c. No charges are made or monies collected for redistribution

3. The electronic version may be printed or the printed version may be photocopied, and the resulting copies used in non-bound format for non-commercial use for the following purposes:

    a. Personal use
    b. Academic or educational use

When reproduced in this way in printed form for academic or educational use, charges may be made to recover actual reproduction and distribution costs but no additional monies may be collected.

4. This book may be republished regionally or locally without royalty by publishers who enter into a relevant micropublishing agreement with Juxta Publishing Limited. Publishers should contact Juxta Publishing Limited in writing to enquire about the Juxta Publishing micropublishing agreement. Without entering into a micropublishing agreement, this book cannot be republished by other publishers.

*Any other reproduction or redistribution in any format is forbidden without the expressed written consent of Juxta Publishing Limited.*

*Had we a thousand lives to live, we could never fully repay Shoghi Effendi with enough love and gratitude for the beauty, inspiration and perfection of his literary work.*

Ugo Giachery, *Shoghi Effendi: Recollections*, p. 42

Photograph by Nayyirih G. de Koning-Tahzib

*In loving memory of*
*Hand of the Cause of God*
*Ugo Giachery*

and

*Lovingly dedicated to*
*my husband Nosrat.*

Through listening to Dr. Giachery speak about Shoghi Effendi and his writings, my great love for Shoghi Effendi and his writings was born and was deepened.

**Shoghi Effendi (3 March 1896 – 4 November 1957)**

*Behold he is this blest and sacred bough that has branched out from the twin holy trees. Well is it with him that seeketh the shelter of his shade that shadoweth all mankind.*

'Abdu'l-Bahá

# Contents

Preface .................................................................................. 17

Acknowledgements .............................................................. 21

Short Biography of Shoghi Effendi ....................................... 23

Understanding Shoghi Effendi's Work ................................. 25

Playing Our Part .................................................................. 29
    1. Bury Our Cares and Teach the Cause ........................... 30
    2. Our Mission Is Most Urgent ......................................... 31
    3. Keep Our Vision Clear .................................................. 32
    4. Live the Life of a True Bahá'í ....................................... 33
    5. The Responsibilities It Is Our Privilege to Shoulder .... 36
    6. Remodel Our Lives ........................................................ 38
    7. Work Towards Universal Redemption ......................... 39
    8. Consciousness of World Citizenship ............................. 40
    9. Direct Our Immediate and Anxious Attention ............ 42
    10. The Requirements of the Present Hour ..................... 44
    11. The Blessings That Will Be Conferred ....................... 45
    12. What We Have to Manifest ......................................... 46
    13. The Vital, Ever-Present Need of Deepening in the Faith ......... 48
    14. Momentous Possibilities ............................................. 50
    15. Contribute to Spiritualization and Material Progress .... 52
    16. Set an Example ............................................................ 53
    17. Seize Every Opportunity ............................................. 54
    18. Distinguish Ourselves by Deeds of Heroism .............. 55
    19. All Must Arise ............................................................. 56

Our Path of Service .............................................................. 59
    20. The Foundation That Must Be Firmly Laid in Our Hearts ..... 60
    21. Effectiveness in Serving ............................................... 62
    22. What We Need to Demonstrate to Our Fellow-Countrymen . 63
    23. How to Ensure Success ................................................ 65
    24. The Object of Our Constant Endeavor ...................... 66
    25. To Teach the Cause Is the Ultimate Purpose ............. 67
    26. Be Lovers of Mankind ................................................. 68
    27. Concentrate Our Energies on the Teaching Work ..... 70
    28. Empower the Bahá'í Youth ......................................... 71
    29. Be Ambassadors of the Message of Bahá'u'lláh ......... 72
    30. Extend Our Range of Activities .................................. 74

31. The Magnet That Will Attract the Promised Blessings ............75
32. We Owe a Debt of Gratitude That No One Can Describe .....77
33. What Must Have Precedence over All Other Considerations..79
34. The Universal Recognition of the Cause ................................81
35. We Must Distinguish Our Record of Stewardship .................83
36. The Spiritual Potentialities That Will Empower Us................84
37. Let Us Place Our Share on the Altar of Sacrifice....................85
38. Our Concerted Exertions Must Be Adequate in Range and Quality.86

Coping with Tests and Difficulties...............................................89
39. Severe Mental Tests Will Sweep over the West.......................90
40. The Plight of Mankind ..........................................................91
41. Problems Will Gradually Be Solved .......................................93
42. Be Undismayed .....................................................................94
43. The Promise ..........................................................................95
44. Pursue the Present Plan .........................................................97
45. Be Not Afraid of Any Criticism..............................................98
46. No Sacrifice Can Be Regarded As Too Great .......................100
47. Face the Trials of the Present Hour......................................101
48. Adversity Prepares the Hearts of Men..................................103
49. Arise Without Fear ..............................................................104
50. So Much Depends Upon Us ...............................................105
51. Trials and Disappointments May Tax Our Patience .............107
52. We Must Encounter Critical Stages with Unswerving Resolution 109
53. So Much Hangs on the Fortunes of the Present Plan...........110
54. The Birth of the World Order .............................................112
55. We Are Never to Hesitate.....................................................113
56. The Tribulations Suffered by Their Co-Religionists.............115
57. Our Faith Must Be Indomitable ..........................................116

The Course of Change................................................................ 121
58. Looking Towards the Future................................................122
59. If We Fail To Play Our Part .................................................123
60. The Significance of Our Undertaking..................................125
61. The Goal of a New World Order .........................................127
62. The Bedrock on Which This Administrative Order Is Founded 129
63. Evidences of a Splendid Power ............................................131
64. A New Stage in Concentrated Teaching Activity .................133
65. The Leaven that Must Leaven the Lump .............................135
66. Undreamt of Opportunities Offered ....................................137
67. The One Refuge ..................................................................138
68. We are Destined to Achieve Memorable Victories ...............140
69. Great Work To Be Undertaken in the Future.......................141
70. The Champion-Builders of Bahá'u'lláh's Embryonic Order...143

71. Torch-Bearers of the Light of Divine Guidance ..................... 145
72. Reap the Full Harvest .......................................................... 147
73. Carry on the Torch ............................................................. 148
74. A Still More Convincing Demonstration of Spirit ................ 150
75. A Dedication Reminiscent of the Pledges of the Dawn-Breakers . 152
76. Not To Be Deflected for a Moment ...................................... 153

Abbreviations ................................................................ 157

Bibliography .................................................................. 159

# Preface

The host of letters and messages that Shoghi Effendi wrote to various parts of the Bahá'í World during his thirty-six years as Guardian of the Bahá'í Faith inspired, praised, advised and guided the Bahá'ís in their endeavors. His words, written in eloquent, excellent language, so rich in beauty of style, empowered the Bahá'ís to carry out their mission with confidence, courage and perseverance. "Empowerment is about engaging both the hearts and minds of people so that they can take the opportunities made available to them for increased responsibility."[1] Without his constant support and encouragement, the believers would never have been able to accomplish what they did.

This compilation features extracts that have been selected from a great variety of letters and messages which Shoghi Effendi wrote to various parts of the globe. The extracts highlight how his words empowered the Bahá'ís to carry out and accomplish what was being asked of them with increased capacity, vision and enthusiasm. They also assist those who have not read Shoghi Effendi's writings at any great length to become more familiar with his writings and pen. The extracts illustrate how enlightening the words of Shoghi Effendi are in giving us a greater understanding of world events, clarifying the goal of humanity, the significance of the mission entrusted to the Bahá'ís, the destiny of certain Bahá'í communities and an increased awareness of the role each individual plays in bringing about what is destined for this age.

The compilation is divided into four sections relevant to our daily lives as Bahá'ís and our services to the Faith: Playing Our Part, Our Path of Service, Coping with Tests and Difficulties and The Course of Change. The extracts are arranged chronologically. Actions or events that took place when Shoghi Effendi wrote the extract are indicated at the beginning of the extract.[2] Each section has nineteen extracts. At the end of each extract the reader will find a glossary of difficult words. These definitions are geared to the text to the best ability of the author of the book, and do not necessarily give a full explanation of all possibilities of the words.

---

1. Michael Armstrong, *How To Be An Even Better Manager*, p. 139.
2. The events are taken from *A Basic Bahá'í Chronology*, (Glenn Cameron with Wendi Momen, George Ronald Publisher). Permission was given by George Ronald, Publisher

Even though the extracts are taken from his letters addressed to different National Spiritual Assemblies, Bahá'í communities and individual believers throughout the world, the guiding principles are universal and can be applied to anyone anytime anywhere.

This compilation is also a tool, which, if referred to in times of need, can get us "back on track" by nourishing our minds and souls to more profoundly understand and cope with the changes taking place in the world, in the Faith, in our Bahá'í communities and in our individual lives.

It is my hope that this compilation will serve as an encouragement and incentive to pursue a prolonged, systematic study of Shoghi Effendi's writings, especially for the junior youth and the youth. As the Universal House of Justice wrote in their telex dated 4 August 1987 to the participants of the Youth Conference in Manchester, United Kingdom:

> Essential that youth through prolonged systematic study writings beloved guardian acquire profound understanding operation of forces of decline and growth creating universal ferment in world today and leading mankind forward to glorious destiny.

Joanna M. Tahzib-Thomas

Photograph by Nayyirih G. de Koning-Tahzib

# Acknowledgements

I wish to express my deepest gratitude to Mr. ʿAli Nakhjávání for his invaluable advice and encouragement. I also want to thank Mr. Robert Weinberg, Mr. Pieter Bas Ruiter and Mr. Jan Folkema for their excellent suggestions. My heartfelt thanks to my daughters: Bahia Tahzib-Lie for her helpful advice and corrections and Nayyirih de Koning-Tahzib for her beautiful photographs. My warmest thanks to Ms. Ruth Borah for her excellent copy-editing and Mrs. Annette Poort and Mr. Herman Poort for reviewing the book and their valuable suggestions. And many thanks to my brother-in-law, Mr. Massoud Tahzib, for his great help in rendering the compilation in book form.

My appreciative thanks to Dr. Wendi Momen for her kind permission to quote from A Basic Baháʾí Dictionary as well as to use information from A Basic Baháʾí Chronology by Glenn Cameron with Wendi Momen. My warm thanks also to George Ronald, Publisher, for their allowing me to quote from Shoghi Effendi: *Recollections* by Ugo Giachery. And lastly, my everlasting gratitude to my husband Nosrat, for his constant encouragement, patience and support.

Joanna M. Tahzib-Thomas

Photograph by Nayyirih G. de Koning-Tahzib

# Short Biography of Shoghi Effendi[3]

The Guardian of the Baháʾí Faith, born on 1 March 1897 in ʿAkká, was the son of Díyáʾíyyih Khánum, the eldest daughter of ʿAbduʾl-Bahá, and Mírzá Hádí Shírazí, a relative of the Báb. He was educated at the American University at Beirut and Balliol College, Oxford.

While at Oxford, Shoghi Effendi was informed of the passing of ʿAbduʾl-Bahá and hurried back to Haifa, where he learned that he had been appointed Guardian of the Cause of God in ʿAbduʾl-Baháʾs Will and Testament:

> After the passing away of this wronged one, it is incumbent upon the Aghsán, the Afnán of the Sacred Lote-Tree, the Hands of the Cause of God and the loved ones of the Abhá Beauty to turn unto Shoghi Effendi ... as he is the sign of God, the chosen branch, the guardian of the Cause of God ... He is the expounder of the words of God ...

Unable to bear his grief over the passing of ʿAbduʾl-Bahá and crushed by the weight of the responsibilities so unexpectedly thrust upon him, Shoghi Effendi retired for some time from Haifa leaving Bahíyyih Khánum in charge. After about a year he returned to take up his office. He married Mary Maxwell, Amatuʾl-Bahá Rúhíyyih Khánum, in 1937.

Among the achievements of his ministry, the following stand out as the most notable: the establishment of the Administrative Order of the Baháʾí Faith (both its elected bodies and the appointed side of the administration); the spread of the Faith to all parts of the globe in a series of organized Plans; the elaboration of many aspects of the Faith and the guidance of the world Baháʾí community through the writing of numerous letters; the defence of the Faith from the actions of the Covenant-breakers; the translation of numerous passages from the Writings of Baháʾuʾlláh; the writing of books such as *God Passes By* and the translation of *Nabíl's Narrative;* the acquisition of land and the planning and supervision of the laying out of the Baháʾí gardens in the Haifa-ʿAkká area; the supervision of the building of the Shrine of the Báb and the International Archives Building.

Shoghi Effendi passed away on 5 November 1957 while in London and is buried in the New Southgate Cemetery there.[4]

---

3. Taken from *A Basic Baháʾí Dictionary*, pp. 208–9 [endnote 16 ommitted].
4. Permission given by George Ronald, Publisher, and Wendi Momen, Author/Writer.

# Understanding Shoghi Effendi's Work

Hand of the Cause, Ugo Giachery, wrote the following in his book *Shoghi Effendi: Recollections* which greatly aids us in understanding Shoghi Effendi's work:

To be able to understand Shoghi Effendi's work, one must realize what animated him to accomplish the titanic task he did. The laws of genetics will perhaps prove that, as the great-grandson of Baha'u'llah, he had inherited many virtues and noble characteristics which made possible his grasp of far greater powers than are available to the average human being, as well as a discernment and spiritual penetration seldom encountered in the most brilliant writer or statesman.

But the true animating forces which permeated all his writings can be placed in three classes. The first was his great vision. With all his passion and zeal he projected himself into the far, far distant future, visualizing the blessings which the World Order of Baha'u'llah would bring to mankind. Often we saw his dear face illumined by the glow of an inner consuming fire, reflecting the glory of this Order, while with a gentle and convincing voice he would tell of the five-hundred-thousand-year Cycle over which Bahá'u'lláh's Revelation would extend its shield and supremacy.

The second force was his unfaltering conviction of the ultimate triumph of the Faith of Bahá'u'lláh. Shoghi Effendi's life was not an easy one, but not even for an infinitesimal instant did he ever hesitate or delay. 'If I should be influenced by the chaotic condition which exists in the world,' he said one evening at the dinner-table, 'I would remain passive and accomplish nothing.' It was at the crucial time of the post-war period when nearly all countries of the world were in want of statesmanship. this unbounded conviction made him a tower of strength, a haven of refuge, and provided him with the power to accomplish things which by human standards would be considered extremely difficult, even impossible.

The third animating force was his faith in the accomplishments of the Bahá'ís throughout the world. This was one of the most real and precious sources of power to him, almost a talisman, something to be found only in the Bahá'í Faith. Shoghi Effendi was a part of the great body of believers; he was like the lymph in the human body. He was well aware that the co-operation of the believers was essential to the unfoldment of Bahá'u'lláh's divine plan for mankind. Verbally and in his written messages he strongly conveyed his acknowledgement of this active partnership of the believers in whatever he did. It was deeply moving to hear him say: 'We have accomplished this'; 'We shall do that'.

Ugo Giachery, *Shoghi Effendi: Recollections,* pp. 31-32
(George Ronald)

Photograph by Nayyirih G. de Koning-Tahzib

# Playing Our Part

Put your shoulder to the wheel.
*Aesop, Hercules and the Wagoner*
*Greek slave & fable author (620 BC - 560 BC)*

**Each** one of us has something unique we can contribute to the Faith. We often wonder how and what we can do to serve the Faith. In searching for just what we can contribute we need to weigh the various aspects involved and what the Faith needs at this particular time.

This section offers just those guidelines that give a solid basis to whatever we are going to do or are doing at the moment.

## 1. Bury Our Cares and Teach the Cause

**In February** 1923, the keys to the Shrine of Bahá'u'lláh were returned to Shoghi Effendi; he wrote to the Bahá'ís in America, Great Britain, Germany, France, Switzerland, Italy, Japan and Australasia about Bahá'í administration, outlining the process for annual elections of assemblies and called for the establishment of local and national funds. In the same month he wrote this:

> But let us be on our guard - so the Master continually reminds us from His Station on high - lest too much concern in that which is secondary in importance, and too long a preoccupation with the details of our affairs and activities, make us neglectful of the most essential, the most urgent of all our obligations, namely, to bury our cares and teach the Cause, delivering far and wide this Message of Salvation to a sorely-stricken world.
>
> *(12 March 1923, BA 42)*

| | |
|---|---|
| *Bury our cares* | To put problems out of our mind; to blot out |
| *Salvation* | Being saved from danger, loss or harm |
| *Sorely-stricken* | Extemely troubled |

## 2. Our Mission Is Most Urgent

In 1923, shortly after Shoghi Effendi returned from Switzerland, the first Local Spiritual Assembly in Australia was formed in Melbourne. Shoghi Effendi wrote to the Bahá'ís of Australia and New Zealand:

> Let us pray to God that in these days of world encircling gloom, when the dark forces of nature, of hate, rebellion, anarchy and reaction are threatening the very stability of human society, when the most precious fruits of civilization are undergoing severe and unparalleled tests, we may all realize, more profoundly than ever, that though but a mere handful amidst the seething masses of the world, are in this day the chosen instruments of God's Grace, that our Mission is most urgent and vital to the fate of humanity and, fortified by these sentiments, arise to achieve God's holy purpose for mankind.
>
> *(2 December 1923, LAN 3)*

| | |
|---|---|
| *Gloom* | An atmosphere of despair, despondency or misery |
| *Anarchy* | A situation in which there is a total lack of organization or control |
| *Severe* | Difficult to do or endure |
| *Unparalleled* | Not equaled, matched or paralleled in kind or quality |
| *Profoundly* | Showing great perception, understanding or knowledge |
| *Mere* | The smallest |
| *Seething* | To be violently agitated or disturbed |
| *Grace* | Generosity of spirit |
| *Vital* | Extremely important and necessary; dispensable to the survival or continuing effectiveness of something |
| *Fate* | A consequence or final result |
| *Fortified* | Strengthened or encouraged |
| *Sentiments* | Underlying feelings |

## 3. Keep Our Vision Clear

**In 1924,** shortly after Shoghi Effendi returned to the Holy Land after an absence of some six months, he wrote to the English National Spiritual Assembly:

> If we all choose to tread faithfully His path, surely the day is not far distant when our beloved Cause will have emerged from the inevitable obscurity of a young and struggling Faith into the broad daylight of universal recognition. This is our duty, our first obligation. Therein lies the secret of the success of the Cause we love so well. Therein lies the hope, the salvation of mankind. Are we fully conscious of our responsibilities? Do we realise the urgency, the sacredness, the immensity, the glory of our task?
>
> I entreat you, dear friends, to continue, nay, to redouble your efforts, to keep your vision clear, your hopes undimmed, your determination unshaken, so that the power of God within us may fill the world with all its glory.
>
> *(24 November 1924, UD 35-36)*

| | |
|---|---|
| *Tread* | Walk |
| *Emerged* | Become known |
| *Inevitable* | Unavoidable |
| *Obscurity* | A state of being unknown or inconspicuous |
| *Immensity* | Unable to be measured; enormous |
| *Unshaken* | Steadfast and unwavering |

## 4. Live the Life of a True Bahá'í

**In November** 1924, the Supreme Court of Iraq decided against the Bahá'ís in the dispute over the House of Bahá'u'lláh in Baghdad. Shoghi Effendi wrote to the English National Spiritual Assembly:

> We have but to turn our eyes to the world without to realise the fierceness and the magnitude of the forces of darkness that are struggling with the dawning light of the Abhá Revelation. Nations, though exhausted and disillusioned, have seemingly begun to cherish anew the spirit of revenge, of domination, and strife. Peoples, convulsed by economic upheavals, are slowly drifting into two great opposing camps with all their menace of social chaos, class hatreds, and world-wide ruin. Races, alienated more than ever before, are filled with mistrust, humiliation and fear, and seem to prepare themselves for a fresh and fateful encounter. Creeds and religions, caught in this whirlpool of conflict and passion, appear to gaze with impotence and despair at this spectacle of increasing turmoil.
>
> Such is the plight of mankind three years after the passing of Him from Whose lips fell unceasingly the sure message of a fast-approaching Divine salvation. Are we by our thoughts, our words, our deeds, whether individually or collectively, preparing the way? Are we hastening the advent of the Day He so often foretold?
>
> None can deny that the flame of faith and love which His mighty hand kindled in many hearts has, despite our bereavement, continued to burn as brightly and steadily as ever before. Who can question that His loved ones, both in the East and the West, notwithstanding the insidious strivings of the enemies of the Cause, have displayed a spirit of unshakable loyalty worthy of the highest praise? What greater perseverance and fortitude than that which His tried and trusted friends have shown in the face of untold calamities, intolerable oppression, and incredible restrictions? Such staunchness of faith, such an unsullied love, such magnificent loyalty, such heroic constancy, such noble courage, however unprecedented and laudable in themselves, cannot alone lead us to the final and complete triumph of such a great Cause. Not until the dynamic love we cherish for Him is sufficiently reflected in its power and purity in all our dealings with our fellowmen, however remotely connected and humble in origin, can we hope to exalt in the eyes of a self-seeking world the genuineness of the all-conquering love of God. Not until we live ourselves the life of a true Bahá'í can we hope to demonstrate the creative and transforming potency of the Faith we profess. Nothing but the abundance of our actions, nothing but the purity of our lives and the integrity of our character, can in the last resort establish our

claim that the Bahá'í spirit is in this day the sole agency that can translate a long cherished ideal into an enduring achievement.

*(24 November 1924, UD 33-34)*

| | |
|---|---|
| *Without* | Outside ourselves; outside our direct surroundings |
| *Fierceness* | Characterized by the violence or intensity of the forces, activity or participants involved |
| *Magnitude* | Greatness of size, volume or extent |
| *Disillusioned* | Disappointed by destroyed illusion |
| *Cherish* | To value something highly, for example, as a right, freedom or privilege |
| *Convulsed* | To cause extreme disruption or disturbance in something |
| *Menace* | Something that is a constant source of trouble and annoyance |
| *Alienated* | To make somebody feel that he or she does not belong to or share in something, or is isolated from it |
| *Gaze* | A long, steady look or stare |
| *Impotence* | The lack of strength or power to do anything |
| *Despair* | A profound feeling that there is no hope |
| *Spectacle* | Some strange or remarkable sight, an unusual display |
| *Turmoil* | A state of great confusion, commotion or disturbance |
| *Plight* | A difficult or dangerous situation, especially a sad or desperate predicament |
| *Unceasingly* | Not stopping; continuous |
| *Salvation* | The saving of somebody or something from harm, destruction, difficulty o failure |
| *Kindled* | To make something glow, or to become bright |
| *Despite* | Notwithstanding or regardless of something |
| *Bereavement* | To deprive somebody of a beloved erson or a treasured thing, especially through death |
| *Notwithstanding* | In spite of |
| *Insidious* | Slowly and subtly harmful or destructive |
| *Fortitud* | Strength and endurance in a difficult or painful situation |
| *Untold* | Too great or numerous to be properly described or counted |
| *Intolerable* | So bad, difficult or painful that it cannot be endured |

| | |
|---|---|
| *Staunchness* | Showing loyalty, dependability and enthusiasm |
| *Unsullied* | Not spoiled or tarnished |
| *Magnificent* | Exceptionally good of its kind; excellent |
| *Unprecedented* | Having no earlier parallel or equivalent |
| *Laudable* | Admirable and worthy of praise |
| *Cherish* | To feel great love or care for somebody |
| *Sufficiently* | As much as is needed |
| *Profess* | To acknowledge something publicly |
| *Abundance* | A great or plentiful amount of something |
| *Integrity* | The quality of possessing and steadfastly adhering to high moral principles or professional standards |
| *Claim* | A statement that something is the case |
| *Sole* | Only; single |
| *Agency* | The action, medium, or means by which something is accomplished |
| *Enduring* | Lasting |

## 5. The Responsibilities It Is Our Privilege to Shoulder

**Two** months after Shoghi Effendi's translation of Nabíl's Narrative entitled 'The Dawnbreakers' was published in 1932, he wrote to the Bahá'ís of the United States and Canada:

> Who, contemplating the helplessness, the fears and miseries of humanity in this day, can any longer question the necessity for a fresh revelation of the quickening power of God's redemptive love and guidance? Who, witnessing on one hand the stupendous advance achieved in the realm of human knowledge, of power, of skill and inventiveness, and viewing on the other the unprecedented character of the sufferings that afflict, and the dangers that beset, present-day society, can be so blind as to doubt that the hour has at last struck for the advent of a new Revelation, for a re-statement of the Divine Purpose, and for the consequent revival of those spiritual forces that have, at fixed intervals, rehabilitated the fortunes of human society?
>
> Does not the very operation of the world-unifying forces that are at work in this age necessitate that He Who is the Bearer of the Message of God in this day should not only reaffirm that self-same exalted standard of individual conduct inculcated by the Prophets gone before Him, but embody in His appeal, to all governments and peoples, the essentials of that social code, that Divine Economy, which must guide humanity's concerted efforts in establishing that all-embracing federation which is to signalize the advent of the Kingdom of God on this earth?
>
> May we not, therefore, recognizing as we do the necessity for such a revelation of God's redeeming power, meditate upon the supreme grandeur of the System unfolded by the hand of Bahá'u'lláh in this day? May we not pause, pressed though we be by the daily preoccupations which the ever-widening range of the administrative activities of His Faith must involve, to reflect upon the sanctity of the responsibilities it is our privilege to shoulder?
>
> (21 March 1932, WOB 60-61)

| | |
|---|---|
| *Stupendous* | Great in extent or degree |
| *Beset* | Trouble continually |
| *Rehabilitated* | Restored to a good condition, state or way of living |
| *Inculcated* | Fixed firmly in someone's mind through forceful repetition |
| *Embody* | To gather and organize a number of things into a whole |

| | |
|---|---|
| *Concerted* | Achieved or performed together |
| *Supreme* | Highest in degree; ultimate |
| *Grandeur* | The quality of being great and very impressive |
| *Sanctity* | Considered holy or sacred; entitled to respect and reverence |

## 6. Remodel Our Lives

**In 1934,** less than a month after Shoghi Effendi gave Queen Marie of Romania the gift of a Tablet in the handwriting of Bahá'u'lláh, he wrote to the Bahá'ís of the West:

> The onrushing forces so miraculously released through the agency of two independent and swiftly successive Manifestations are now under our very eyes and through the care of the chosen stewards of a far-flung Faith being gradually mustered and disciplined. They are slowly crystallizing into institutions that will come to be regarded as the hall-mark and glory of the age we are called upon to establish and by our deeds immortalize. For upon our present-day efforts, and above all upon the extent to which we strive to remodel our lives after the pattern of sublime heroism associated with those gone before us, must depend the efficacy of the instruments we now fashion - instruments that must erect the structure of that blissful Commonwealth which must signalize the Golden Age of our Faith.
>
> *(8 February 1934, WOB 98)*

| | |
|---|---|
| *Onrushing* | Rushing forward or onward |
| *Successive* | Following one another |
| *Stewards* | Those who actively direct affairs |
| *Far-flung* | Widely distributed; wide-ranging |
| *Mustered* | Gathered together for a particular reason |
| *Crystallizing* | Taking a definite form |
| *Hall-mark* | A distinguishing characteristic, trait or feature |
| *Immortalize* | To make eternal |
| *Extent* | The degree to which something applies |
| *Strive* | To try hard to achieve or get something |
| *Sublime* | Of the highest moral or spiritual value |
| *Efficacy* | The ability to produce the necessary or desired results |
| *Fashion* | To give form or shape to something |
| *Blissful* | Characterized by perfect happiness |
| *Commonwealth* | A nation or state governed by the people |
| *Signalize* | To make something conspicuous or remarkable |

## 7. Work Towards Universal Redemption

Just a half year after Queen Marie of Romania died, Shoghi Effendi penned these words in 1938 to the Bahá'ís of the United States and Canada:

> So sad and moving a spectacle, bewildering as it must be to every observer unaware of the purposes, the prophecies, and promises of Bahá'u'lláh, far from casting dismay into the hearts of His followers, or paralyzing their efforts, cannot but deepen their faith, and excite their enthusiastic eagerness to arise and display, in the vast field traced for them by the pen of 'Abdu'l-Bahá, their capacity to play their part in the work of universal redemption proclaimed by Bahá'u'lláh.
>
> *(25 December 1938, ADJ 39-40)*

| | |
|---|---|
| *Spectacle* | Some strange or remarkable sight, an unusual display |
| *Casting* | Causing to fall into a certain state |
| *Dismay* | A complete loss of courage in the face of trouble |
| *Redemption* | Improving something that has declined into a poor state |

## 8. Consciousness of World Citizenship

In 1939, four months before World War II began with Britain and France declaring war on Germany after Germany invaded Poland, Shoghi Effendi wrote to the Bahá'ís of North America:

> Far be it from me to underrate the gigantic proportions of their task, nor do I for one moment overlook the urgency and gravity of the times in which they are laboring. Nor do I wish to minimize the hazards and trials that surround or lie ahead of them. The grandeur of their task is indeed commensurate with the mortal perils by which their generation is hemmed in.
>
> As the dusk creeps over a steadily sinking society the radiant outlines of their redemptive mission become sharper every day. The present world unrest, symptom of a world-wide malady, their world religion has already affirmed must needs culminate in that world catastrophe out of which the consciousness of world citizenship will be born, a consciousness that can alone provide an adequate basis for the organization of world unity, on which a lasting world peace must necessarily depend, the peace itself inaugurating in turn that world civilization which will mark the coming of age of the entire human race.
>
> Fortified by such reflections, the American believers, in whichever section of the Western Hemisphere they find themselves laboring, whether at home or abroad, and however dire and distressing the processes involved in the disintegration of the structure of present-day civilization, will, I feel convinced, prove themselves, through their lives and deeds, worthy of that priceless heritage which it is their undoubted privilege to proclaim, preserve and perpetuate.
>
> *(22 May 1939, MA 45)*

| | |
|---|---|
| *Underrate* | To judge the value, degree or worth of someone or something to be less than it really is |
| *Gravity* | The seriousness of something considered in terms of its unfavorable consequences |
| *Hazards* | Possible sources of danger |
| *Grandeur* | The quality of being great or grand, and very impressive |
| *Commensurate* | Of the same size or extent |
| *Mortal* | Marked by great intensity or severity |
| *Hemmed in* | Surrounded and enclosed |
| *Dusk* | Partial or almost complete darkness |
| *Creeps* | To appear, approach or develop gradually |

| | |
|---|---|
| *Outlines* | A preliminary account of a project |
| *Redemptive:* | Saving someone or something from error or evil |
| *Malady* | Sickness; an unwholesome condition that equires a remedy |
| *Culminate* | Reach a climax; come to completion |
| *Catastrophe* | An occurrence causing widespread destruction and distress |
| *Inaugurating* | To initiate something or put it into operation, especially in a formal or official manner |
| *Coming of age* | Reaching an advanced stage of development |
| *Fortified* | Strengthened; encouraged |
| *Reflections* | Careful thought, especially the process of reconsidering previous actions, events or decisions |
| *Dire* | Characterized by severe, serious or desperate circumstances |
| *Distressing* | Causing someone to feel extremely upset |
| *Processes* | A series of actions directed toward a specific aim |
| *Disintegration* | The loss of unity, cohesion, or integrity |
| *Structure* | A system or organization made up of interrelated parts functioning as a whole |
| *Perpetuate* | To make something continue, usually for a very long time |

## 9. Direct Our Immediate and Anxious Attention

In 1939, Shoghi Effendi ordered from Italy twin monuments similar in style to that of the Greatest Holy Leaf and sought permission from the British authorities to reinter the remains of Navváb and the Purest Branch on Mount Carmel near those of Bahiyyíh Khanum and the Holy Mother. He wrote to the American Bahá'í community in the summer:

> ... It is to the fierce struggle, the imperious duties, the distinctive contributions which the present generation of Bahá'ís are summoned to undertake and render that I feel we should, at this hour, direct our immediate and anxious attention. Though powerless to avert the impending contest the followers of Bahá'u'lláh can, by the spirit they evince and the efforts they exert help to circumscribe its range, shorten its duration, allay its hardships, proclaim its salutary consequences, and demonstrate its necessary and vital role in the shaping of human destiny. Theirs is the duty to hold, aloft and undimmed, the torch of Divine guidance, as the shades of night descend upon, and ultimately envelop the entire human race. Theirs is the function, amidst its tumults, perils and agonies, to witness to the vision, and proclaim the approach, of that re-created society, that Christ-promised Kingdom, that World Order whose generative impulse is the spirit of none other than Bahá'u'lláh Himself, whose dominion is the entire planet, whose watchword is unity, whose animating power is the force of Justice, whose directive purpose is the reign of righteousness and truth, and whose supreme glory is the complete, the undisturbed and everlasting felicity of the whole of human kind. By the sublimity and serenity of their faith, by the steadiness and clarity of their vision, the incorruptibility of their character, the rigor of their discipline, the sanctity of their morals, and the unique example of their community life, they can and indeed must in a world polluted with its incurable corruptions, paralyzed by its haunting fears, torn by its devastating hatreds, and languishing under the weight of its appalling miseries demonstrate the validity of their claim to be regarded as the sole repository of that grace upon whose operation must depend the complete deliverance, the fundamental reorganization and the supreme felicity of all mankind.
>
> *(28 July 1939, MA 50)*

| | |
|---|---|
| *Fierce* | Violent or intense |
| *Imperious* | Urgent; pressing |
| *Distinctive* | Individually characteristic; different from others |
| *Summoned* | Called upon for specific action |

| | |
|---|---|
| *Render* | Provide or give |
| *Avert* | To prevent something from occurring |
| *Impending* | About to happen |
| *Evince* | To show a feeling or a quality clearly |
| *Exert* | Apply or bring to bear |
| *Circumscribe* | To limit something |
| *Allay* | To reduce the intensity of; relieve |
| *Salutary* | Of value or benefit to somebody or something |
| *Aloft* | Upwards, high up, or in a higher position |
| *Animating* | Arousing somebody or something into activity |
| *Felicity* | Great happiness; bliss |
| *Sublimity* | Excellence; being particularly impressive |
| *Clarity* | Clearness in what somebody is thinking |
| *Incorruptibility* | Incapable of being morally corrupted, especially incapable of being bribed or motivated by selfish interests |
| *Rigor* | Forcefulness or extremely strict obedience to rules |
| *Sanctity* | The condition of being considered sacred or holy, and therefore entitled to respect and reverence |
| *Haunting* | Evoking strong emotion, specially a sense of sadness, that persists for a long time |
| *Devastating* | Causing severe or widespread damage |
| *Languishing* | Existing in miserable or disheartening conditions, often as a result of being deprived of independence, freedom or attention |
| *Appalling* | Shocking and very bad |
| *Validity* | Based on truth or reason; able to be accepted |
| *Sole* | Only; single |
| *Repository* | Entrusted with something special |
| *Fundamental* | Basic or central |
| *Supreme* | Highest in degree |

## 10. The Requirements of the Present Hour

**In 1941,** when Shaykh Kázim was martyred, Ridá Shah abdicated and Muhammad-Ridá Shah acceded to the throne of Iran. Soon after, Shoghi Effendi wrote to the National Spiritual Assembly of India:

> … The vastness of the field, the smallness of your numbers, the indifference of the masses, must neither discourage nor appal you. You should at all times fix your gaze on the promise of Bahá'u'lláh, put your whole trust in His creative Word, recall the past and manifold evidences of His all-encompassing and resistless power and arise to become worthy and exemplary recipients of His all-sustaining grace and blessings. I appeal to every Indian and Burmese believer, however modest his position, however limited his knowledge, however restricted his means, to rise to the height of this great opportunity which if missed will not recur again. To disperse, to settle, to teach by word and deed, to persevere and sacrifice are the requirements of the present hour. May the Almighty, Whose Cause you are labouring to advance, endow you and your fellow-workers with all the wisdom, the strength, and guidance that you need to acquit yourselves worthily of this task.
>
> *(29 June 1941, DND 90-91)*

| | |
|---|---|
| *Vastness* | Very great in size, amount, extent, number or degree |
| *Appal* | Dismay or shock |
| *Gaze* | A steady, fixed look with unwavering attention |
| *Manifold* | Many and various |
| *Restricted* | Limited |
| *Recur* | Occur again |
| *Acquit* | Behave or perform in a specified way |

## 11. The Blessings That Will Be Conferred

In 1947, the United Nations Committee on Palestine requested a statement on the relationship between the Bahá'í Faith and the Bahá'í attitude to any future changes in the status of the country. Shoghi Effendi replied, setting out the non-political character of the Bahá'í Faith and explaining that Palestine is both the administrative and the spiritual headquarters of the religion. Several months later he wrote to the British National Assembly:

> The gigantic task, now being so energetically and successfully carried out by the consecrated and firmly knit British Bahá'í community, constitutes a glorious landmark in recent Bahá'í history, and will, when viewed in proper perspective, deserve to be regarded as one of the most outstanding enterprises launched by the followers of Bahá'u'lláh in the opening years of the second Bahá'í century. Alike in its magnitude and significance, this momentous undertaking is unprecedented in the annals of the Faith in the British Isles, and deserves to rank as one of the most compelling evidences of the creative power of its Author, marking the rise and establishment of His institutions on the European continent. It is yet too early to assess the potentialities of this present Plan and those destined to follow it, or estimate their future benefits. The blessings they will confer, as the forces latent within them are progressively revealed, on the people dwelling within those Islands, and subsequently, as their sphere is enlarged and their implications are fully disclosed, on the diversified peoples and races inhabiting the widely scattered dependencies of a far-flung empire, in both the East and the West, are unimaginably glorious.
>
> (24 October 1947, UD 208)

| | |
|---|---|
| *Consecrated* | Dedicated to a sacred purpose |
| *Firmly knit* | Securely united |
| *Constitutes* | Creates or establishes something formally |
| *Landmark* | Important new development |
| *Rank* | To give a particular order or status to something |
| *Compelling* | Attracting strong interest and attention |
| *Latent* | Present, but not evident or active |
| *Implications* | Consequences; influences |

## 12. What We Have to Manifest

**In 1948,** when the owners of a house near the Shrine of Bahá'u'lláh fled and the house became government property, Shoghi Effendi restored the house and made it into a pilgrim house. In the same year, he wrote to the American Bahá'í Community:

> May He Who called them into being and raised them up, Who fostered them in their infancy, Who extended to them the blessing of His personal support in their years of childhood, Who bequeathed to them the distinguishing heritage of His Plan, Whose Will and Testament initiated them, during the period of their adolescence, in the processes of a divinely appointed Administrative Order, Who enabled them to attain maturity through the inauguration of the first stage in the execution of His Plan, Who conferred upon them the privilege of spiritual parenthood at the close of the initial phase in the operation of that same Plan, continue through the further unfoldment of the second stage in its evolution to guide their steps along the path leading to the assumption of functions proclaiming the attainment of full spiritual manhood, and enable them eventually, through the long and slow processes of evolution and in conformity with the future requirements of a continually evolving Plan, to manifest before the eyes of the members of their sister communities, their countrymen and the whole world, and in all their plenitude, the potentialities inherent within them, and which in the fullness of time, must reflect in its perfected form, the glories of the mission constituting their birthright.
>
> *(8 November 1948, CF 63)*

| | |
|---|---|
| *Fostered* | Promoted the growth or development of |
| *Bequeathed* | Handed something down to future generations, for example, knowledge or practice, |
| *Distinguishing* | Special; different |
| *Heritage* | Property that is passed down |
| *Initiated* | Instructed in the principles of something new |
| *Enabled* | Provided somebody with the resources, authority or opportunity to do something |
| *Attain* | To achieve a goal or desired state, usually with effort |
| *Inauguration* | The act of bringing something into service or putting it into operation |
| *Conferred* | To give, to grant |
| *Assumption* | Taking something upon yourself |
| *Conformity* | Following a standard |

| | |
|---|---|
| *Manifest* | To show something clearly |
| *Plenitude* | An abundance or plentiful supply of something |
| *Inherent* | Existing as a natural or basic part of something |
| *Fullness* | The quality of being full or complete |
| *Constituting* | Amounting to, or having the status of a particular thing |
| *Birthright* | A right or privilege to which a person is entitled by birth |

## 13. The Vital, Ever-Present Need of Deepening in the Faith

The name 'Bahá'í International Community' was first used in March 1948 to refer to the eight existing National Spiritual Assemblies. They were recognized collectively as a non-governmental organization which took part in its first United Nations conference in May, on human rights. Later that year, Shoghi Effendi wrote to the National Spiritual Assembly of Australia and New Zealand:

> As the processes impelling a rapidly evolving Order on the highroad of its destiny multiply and gather momentum, attention should be increasingly directed to the vital need of ensuring, by every means possible, the deepening of the Faith, the understanding and the spiritual life of the individuals who, as the privileged members of this community, are called upon to participate in this glorious unfoldment, and are lending their assistance to this historic evolution. A profound study of the Faith which they have espoused, its history, its spiritual as well as administrative principles; a thorough understanding of the Covenant of Bahá'u'lláh and of the Will of 'Abdu'l-Bahá, a deeper realization of the implications of the claims advanced by the Founders of the Faith; strict adherence to the laws and principles which they have established; a greater dedication to the fundamentals and verities enshrined in their teachings - these constitute, I feel convinced, the urgent need of the members of this rapidly expanding community. For upon this spiritual foundation must depend the solidity of the institutions which they are now so painstakingly erecting. Every outward thrust into new fields, every multiplication of Bahá'í institutions, must be paralleled by a deeper thrust of the roots which sustain the spiritual life of the community and ensure its sound development. From this vital, this ever-present need, attention must at no time be diverted; nor must it be, under any circumstances, neglected, or subordinated to the no less vital and urgent task of ensuring the outer expansion of Bahá'í administrative institutions. That this community, so alive, so devoted, so strikingly and rapidly developing, may maintain a proper balance between these two essential aspects of its development, and march forward with rapid strides and along sound lines toward the goal of the Plan it has adopted, is the ardent hope of my heart and my constant prayer.
>
> *(30 December 1948, LAN 75-76)*

| | |
|---|---|
| *Impelling* | Starting or keeping something or somebody moving in a particular direction |
| *Highroad* | The easiest or most direct way to somewhere |
| *Ensuring* | Making sure that something will happen |

| | |
|---|---|
| *Espoused* | Adopted or supported something as a belief or cause |
| *Implications* | The effects that an action or decision will have on something else in the future |
| *Adherence* | Holding firmly to a belief, idea or opinion |
| *Enshrined* | Cherished as sacred |
| *Constitute* | To make up the whole or a particular part of something |
| *Solidity* | Being solid and reliable |
| *Painstakingly* | Carefully and with attention to detail |
| *Thrust* | A forceful movement or push |
| *Sustain* | To make something continue to exist; support |
| *Ensure* | To make sure that something will happen or be available |
| *Diverted* | Distracted; turned aside from a course of action |
| *Subordinated* | Treating something as less important and allowing something else to take priority |
| *Strikingly* | Attracting attention, especially in an impressive or unusual way |

## 14. Momentous Possibilities

In 1949, during the month when the second European Teaching Conference was held in Brussels, Belgium, Shoghi Effendi wrote to the National Assembly of Australia and New Zealand:

> The task undertaken is immense, fraught with momentous possibilities, highly delicate in nature, and bound to have far-reaching repercussions, not only in the West, and particularly in the continent of Europe, where the institutions of Bahá'u'lláh's Administrative Order are emerging with such rapidity and showing such promise, but on the continent of Asia, where the overwhelming majority of the followers of the Most Great Name, have endured such grievous afflictions, and are faced with grave peril, and are battling so heroically against the forces of darkness with which they are encompassed. The nature of the work in which this wide-awake, untrammelled unprejudiced, freedom-loving community, is so energetically engaged, cannot, therefore, be regarded as a purely local and isolated enterprise, but is vitally linked with the fortunes of a world-encircling Order, functioning mysteriously in both the Eastern and Western Hemispheres, highly organized in its administrative machinery, sensitive in its mechanism, far-flung in its ramifications, challenging in its features, revolutionizing in its implications, and destined to seek increasingly, as it expands and develops, the goodwill and assistance of the civil authorities in every continent of the globe.
>
> *(22 August 1949, LAN 79-80)*

| | |
|---|---|
| *Fraught* | Full of or charged with a particular element |
| *Repercussions* | Widespread, indirect or unforeseen effects of an act, action or event |
| *Emerging* | Starting to appear, arise, occur or develop |
| *Endured* | Experienced exertion, pain or hardship without giving up |
| *Grievous* | Very bad or severe |
| *Afflictions* | Conditions of great physical or mental distress |
| *Grave* | Likely to produce great harm or danger |
| *Peril* | Danger, exposure to risk of harm |
| *Encompassed* | Surrounded, enveloped or encircled |
| *Untrammelled* | Not restricted or restrained |
| *Enterprise* | A project or undertaking that is especially difficult, complicated or risky |
| *Vitally* | Of the utmost importance; essentially |
| *Fortunes* | The success or failure of a person or enterprise |

| | |
|---|---|
| *Far-flung* | Widespread |
| *Ramifications* | The possible results of an action |
| *Challenging* | Difficult, in a way that tests your ability or determination |
| *Features* | Important elements of something |
| *Revolutionizing* | Causing a radical change in something such as a method or approach |
| *Implications* | Important and extensive effects |

## 15. Contribute to Spiritualization and Material Progress

In 1951, after Shoghi Effendi announced the establishment of the International Bahá'í Council (a forerunner to the Universal House of Justice) with its seat in the Western Pilgrim House, and also one day before he announced the completion of the restoration of the House of ʽAbbúd, he wrote to the National Spiritual Assembly of Canada:

> May this community, the leaven placed by the hands of Providence in the midst of a people belonging to a nation, likewise young dynamic, richly endowed with material resources, and assured of a great material prosperity by 'Abdu'l-Bahá, play its part not only in lending a notable impetus to the world-wide propagation of the Faith it has espoused, but contribute, as its resources multiply and as it gains in stature, to the spiritualization and material progress of the nation of which it forms so vital a part.
>
> *(1 March 1951, MC 23)*

| | |
|---|---|
| *Leaven* | An element or agent that works to lighten or modify a whole (like yeast in bread) |
| *Providence* | God, perceived as a caring force guiding humankind |
| *Lending* | Giving a particular quality or character to something |
| *Notable* | Significant, interesting or unusual enough to deserve attention or to be recorded |
| *Impetus* | The energy or motivation to accomplish or undertake something |

## 16. Set an Example

In 1952, Shoghi Effendi appointed the second contingent of Hands of the Cause of God; described the plans for a marble colonnade to encircle the Shrine of the Báb as an intermediate step to building a superstructure for the Shrine; sent his ideas to Italy for scale drawings and a cost estimate; and also announced the enlargement of the International Bahá'í Council to eight members. It was in this year that he wrote to the German National Spiritual Assembly:

> Time is running out. The work they have to accomplish is immense, exacting, thrilling and inescapable. The hosts of the Concourse on high will surely lead them onward and assure them a resounding victory, if they but keep their vision undimmed, if they refuse to faint or falter, if they persevere and remain faithful to both the spiritual and the administrative principles inculcated by their Faith.
>
> That they may discharge nobly their trust, that they may emerge triumphant from the first stage of their collective and historic undertaking, that they may set an undying example to their brethren in East and West, of Bahá'í solidarity, of tenacity of purpose, of single-minded devotion, of unrelaxing vigilance, of assiduous labour, of harmonious cooperation, of audacity, and of absolute dedication to the aims and purposes of their Faith, is the object of my special, my loving and constant prayers at the threshold of the Shrine of Bahá'u'lláh.
>
> (30 May 1952, LDG Vol. I, 186)

| | |
|---|---|
| *Resounding* | Clear and unmistakable |
| *Inculcated* | Instilled; taught by frequent instruction |
| *Tenacity* | Very determined |
| *Vigilance* | Alert watchfulness |
| *Assiduous* | Something done with constant and careful attention |
| *Audacity* | Willing to take bold risks: daring |

## 17. Seize Every Opportunity

**He addressed** the National Spiritual Assembly of Australia and New Zealand in 1952 shortly before he inaugurated The Holy Year, when he also announced his decision to launch "the fate-laden, soul-stirring, decade-long world-embracing Spiritual Crusade" in the coming year and he called upon the Hands of the Cause to appoint during Riḍván 1954 five Auxiliary Boards to act as their adjuncts or deputies to work with the National Spiritual Assemblies to execute the projected national plans:

> This community, now standing on the threshold of an era of unprecedented expansion, and gazing towards the glorious future that awaits it, must seize the priceless opportunities which these fast-fleeting months offer it, and must not allow for a moment its vision to be dimmed, its resolution to flag, its attention to be distracted or its faith in its ultimate destiny to waver.
>
> With a heart full of hope, and with an affection and fervour which every forward step in the progress of its strenuous labours serves to intensify, I will supplicate at the threshold of the Shrine of Bahá'u'lláh to enable His stalwart followers championing His Cause in those far-away lands to achieve a resounding success in the task they have pledged themselves to fulfil.
>
> *(Shoghi Effendi, June 3, 1952, appended to a letter written on his behalf to the National Spiritual Assembly of Australia and New Zealand, published in "Letters from the Guardian to Australia and New Zealand", p. 106)*

| | |
|---|---|
| *Unprecedented* | Never done or known before |
| *Resolution* | A firm decision to do something |
| *Waver* | To become unsure |
| *Fervour* | Extreme intensity of emotion or belief |
| *Strenuous* | Requiring great effort |
| *Stalwart* | Dependable and loyal |
| *Resounding* | Clear and unmistakable |

## 18. Distinguish Ourselves by Deeds of Heroism

**In April** 1953, Shoghi Effendi, during a moving ceremony, placed a silver box containing a fragment of plaster from the ceiling of the Báb's cell in Máh-Kú under a tile in the golden dome of the Shrine of the Báb. That year he also announced plans to build a House of Worship in Frankfurt, and sent this message to the Hands of the Cause, members of the National Spiritual Assemblies, the pioneers, the resident believers and visitors attending the European Intercontinental Teaching Conference in Stockholm, Sweden, in July:

> May all the privileged participants, enlisting under the banner of Bahá'u'lláh for the promotion of so pre-eminent and meritorious a Cause, be they from the Eastern or Western hemisphere, of either sex, white or coloured, young or old, neophyte or veteran, whether serving in their capacity as expounders of the teachings, or administrators, of His Faith, as settlers or itinerant teachers, distinguish themselves by such deeds of heroism as will rival, nay outshine, the feats accomplished nineteen hundred years ago by that little band of God-intoxicated disciples who, fearlessly preaching the Gospel of a newly-arisen Messiah, contributed so decisively to the illumination, the regeneration and the advancement of the entire European continent.
>
> (21 July 1953, UD 320)

| | |
|---|---|
| *Enlisting* | Becoming actively involved in an effort |
| *Banner* | A guiding principle or cause |
| *Pre-eminent* | Highly distinguished or outstanding |
| *Neophyte* | A recent convert to a religion |
| *Expounders* | Those who give an explanation of the meaning and implications of a written text |
| *Itinerant* | Traveling from place to place |
| *Outshine* | To surpass somebody or something else, especially in terms of excellence or quality |
| *Feats* | Remarkable acts or achievements involving courage, skill or strength |
| *Intoxicated* | Intensely excited |

## 19. All Must Arise

In 1957, three months before Shoghi Effendi wrote to the National Spiritual Assembly of the Benelux Countries, he announced the appointments of the third contingent of Hands of the Cause of God: Enoch Olinga, William Sears, John Robarts, Hasan Balyuzi, John Ferraby, Collis Featherstone, Rahmatu'lláh Muhájir and Abdu'l-Qásim Faizi and designated the Hands of the Cause the "Chief Stewards of Bahá'u'lláh's embryonic World commonwealth"; four months later Shoghi Effendi passed away in London:

> ... No sacrifice can be deemed too great, no labour too arduous. For the purpose of achieving its goals all must arise, whether young or old, however limited their resources or experience, to contribute their share to the consummation of this collective task. A concerted effort, unexampled in its range and intensity, must needs be exerted to augment, to an unprecedented degree, the number of the avowed and active supporters of the Faith in each of these three countries, whose people stand in such dire need of its life-giving principles and ideals as well as its divinely appointed institutions. Simultaneously, effective measures must be undertaken, by the elected representatives of these communities, as well as by the rank and file of the believers, to multiply rapidly the number of isolated centres, groups and local assemblies, constituting the bedrock on which a divinely conceived order must rest.
>
> (5 July 1957, DC 151)

| | |
|---|---|
| *Deemed* | Considered to be |
| *Arduous* | Difficult and tiring |
| *Consummation* | Fulfilment; completion |
| *Concerted* | Achieved or performed together |
| *Augment* | Increase |
| *Avowed* | Openly declared |
| *Dire* | Desperately urgent |
| *Simultaneously* | At the same time |

Photograph by Nayyirih G. de Koning-Tahzib

# Our Path of Service

> Faith is taking the first step, even when you don't see the whole staircase.

**What** does it mean to serve the Faith? How should we view our service to the Faith? How can we become more effective? How important is what we do? And how much time should we give to serving the Faith? These kinds of questions are important to address.

This section sheds light on service and its many aspects.

## 20. The Foundation That Must Be Firmly Laid in Our Hearts

**During** 1923, Amelia Collins contributed the funds necessary to complete the Western Pilgrim House. In the same month that Shoghi Effendi sent his early translation of the "Hidden Words" to America, he wrote to the Bahá'ís throughout London, Manchester and Bournemouth care of the National Spiritual Assembly of the British Isles:

> The supreme necessity, and the urgent need of the Cause of God at present, is the unity of the friends, and their sustained and wholehearted co-operation in their task of spreading the Divine Teachings throughout the world. It is the sacred duty of all believers to have implicit confidence in, and support heartily, every decision passed by their Spiritual Assemblies, whether local or central; and the members of these Assemblies must, on their part, set aside their own inclinations, personal interests, likes and dislikes, and regard only the welfare of the Cause and the well-being of the friends. This is surely the foundation which must be firmly laid in the hearts of all believers the world over, for upon this only can any constructive and permanent service be achieved, and the edifice of the Beloved's last instructions, as revealed in His Will and Testament, be raised and established.
>
> The all-conquering Spirit of Bahá'u'lláh cannot prove effective in this world of strife and turmoil, and cannot achieve its purpose for mankind, unless we, who are named after His Name, and who are the recipients of His Grace, endeavour, by our example, our daily life and our dealings with our fellow-men, to reveal that noble spirit of love and self-sacrifice of which the world stands in need at present.
>
> *(1 February 1923, UD 13-14)*

| | |
|---|---|
| *Supreme* | Greater than or superior to any other, especially above all others in power, authority, rank, status or skill |
| *Sustained* | Kept up; prolonged |
| *Implicit* | Not affected by any uncertainty or doubt; unquestioning |
| *Heartily* | In a full and complete way |
| *Inclinations* | Preferences or tendencies; feelings that make a person want to do one thing instead of another |
| *Welfare* | Prosperity; success |
| *Well-being* | The state of being happy, healthy or prosperous |
| *Edifice* | An elaborate structure |

| | |
|---|---|
| *All-conquering* | Victorious; overcoming obstacles or opposition |
| *Strife* | Bitter and sometimes violent conflict, struggle or rivalry |
| *Turmoil* | A state of great confusion, commotion or disturbance |

## 21. Effectiveness in Serving

**In 1926** in May, Queen Marie of Romania wrote three articles as a testimonial to the Bahá'í Faith for a syndicated series entitled "Queen's Counsel" which appeared in over 200 newspapers in the United States and Canada. Shoghi Effendi wrote this to an individual:

> I strongly urge you to devote, while you are pursuing your studies, as much time as you possibly can to a thorough study of the history and Teachings of our Beloved Cause. This is the prerequisite of a future successful career of service to the Bahá'í Faith in which I hope and pray you will distinguish yourself in the days to come.
>
> *(18 May 1926, CC Vol. II, 416)*

| | |
|---|---|
| *Prerequisite* | An object, quality, or condition that is required in order for something else to happen |

## 22. What We Need to Demonstrate to Our Fellow-Countrymen

In 1927, the National Spiritual Assembly of the United States and Canada drew up and published a "Declaration of Trust" and "By-laws of the National Spiritual Assembly". Shoghi Effendi described it as the Bahá'í "national constitution" heralding "the formation of the constitution of the future Bahá'í World Community". It was also in this year that Shoghi Effendi translated the "Hidden Words" and wrote to the National Spiritual Assembly of the United States and Canada:

> Not by merely imitating the excesses and laxity of the extravagant age they live in; not by the idle neglect of the sacred responsibilities it is their privilege to shoulder; not by the silent compromise of the principles dearly cherished by 'Abdu'l-Bahá; not by their fear of unpopularity or their dread of censure can they hope to rouse society from its spiritual lethargy, and serve as a model to a civilization the foundations of which the corrosion of prejudice has well-nigh undermined. By the sublimity of their principles, the warmth of their love, the spotless purity of their character, and the depth of their devoutness and piety, let them demonstrate to their fellow-countrymen the ennobling reality of a power that shall weld a disrupted world.
>
> We can prove ourselves worthy of our Cause only if in our individual conduct and corporate life we sedulously imitate the example of our beloved Master, Whom the terrors of tyranny, the storms of incessant abuse, the oppressiveness of humiliation, never caused to deviate a hair's breadth from the revealed Law of Bahá'u'lláh.
>
> Such is the path of servitude, such is the way of holiness He chose to tread to the very end of His life. Nothing short of the strictest adherence to His glorious example can safely steer our course amid the pitfalls of this perilous age, and lead us on to fulfill our high destiny.
>
> *(2 April 1927, BA 131-132)*

| | |
|---|---|
| *Rouse* | To stir somebody into action or make them become more active |
| *Lethargy* | Lack of energy, activity or enthusiasm |
| *Piety* | A strong, respectful belief in God and strict observance of religious principles in everyday life |
| *Weld* | To form a union or a close association |

| | |
|---|---|
| *Disrupted* | Destroyed the order or orderly progression of something |
| *Sedulously* | Carried out with great care, concentration and commitment |

## 23. How to Ensure Success

**During** March of 1930, when Queen Marie of Romania's visit to the Bahá'í Shrines was thwarted, Shoghi Effendi wrote to the Bahá'ís of the West the following:

> How pressing and sacred the responsibility that now weighs upon those who are already acquainted with these teachings! How glorious the task of those who are called upon to vindicate their truth, and demonstrate their practicability to an unbelieving world! Nothing short of an immovable conviction in their divine origin, and their uniqueness in the annals of religion; nothing short of an unwavering purpose to execute and apply them to the administrative machinery of the Cause, can be sufficient to establish their reality, and insure their success. How vast is the Revelation of Bahá'u'lláh! How great the magnitude of His blessings showered upon humanity in this day! And yet, how poor, how inadequate our conception of their significance and glory! This generation stands too close to so colossal a Revelation to appreciate, in their full measure, the infinite possibilities of His Faith, the unprecedented character of His Cause, and the mysterious dispensations of His Providence.
>
> *(21 March 1930, WOB 24)*

| | |
|---|---|
| *Pressing* | Needing to be attended to without delay |
| *Vindicate* | Confirm, defend, uphold |
| *Nothing short* | There is no other course of action open to somebody |
| *Unwavering* | Steady and firm in purpose |
| *Machinery* | An interconnected series of parts or processes that works like a mechanical system to produce a result |
| *Vast* | Enormous; very great in size, number or amount |
| *Magnitude* | Greatness of size |
| *Blessings* | God's help |
| *Shower* | A large flow of something; an outpouring |
| *Colossal* | Unusually large |
| *Appreciate* | Value very highly |
| *Full measure* | Highest degree or largest extent |
| *Infinite* | Not measurable |
| *Unprecedented* | Having no earlier parallel or equivalent |
| *Dispensations* | Divine ordering of affairs and events of the world |
| *Providence* | Divine direction; the care, guardianship and control exercised by God |

## 24. The Object of Our Constant Endeavor

**In January** of 1934, Shoghi Effendi gave a gift of a Tablet in the handwriting of Bahá'u'lláh to Queen Marie of Romania. A month later he wrote to the Bahá'ís of the West:

> To strive to obtain a more adequate understanding of the significance of Bahá'u'lláh's stupendous Revelation must, it is my unalterable conviction, remain the first obligation and the object of the constant endeavor of each one of its loyal adherents. An exact and thorough comprehension of so vast a system, so sublime a revelation, so sacred a trust, is for obvious reasons beyond the reach and ken of our finite minds. We can, however, and it is our bounden duty to seek to derive fresh inspiration and added sustenance as we labor for the propagation of His Faith through a clearer apprehension of the truths it enshrines and the principles on which it is based.
>
> *(8 February 1934, WOB 100)*

| | |
|---|---|
| *Strive* | To try hard to achieve or get something |
| *Obtain* | To get possession of something, especially by making an effort or having the necessary qualifications |
| *Significance* | The quality of having importance or being regarded as having great meaning |
| *Stupendous* | Impressively large, excellent or great in extent or degree |
| *Unalterable* | Permanent |
| *Conviction* | Firmly held belief |
| *Adherents* | Supporters |
| *Comprehension* | The grasping of the meaning of something |
| *Sublime* | So awe-inspiringly beautiful as to seem almost heavenly |
| *Trust* | A situation in which things are placed in the care of somebody who is expected to behave responsibly and honorably |
| *Reach and ken* | Understanding; perception |
| *Bounden* | Morally binding; obligatory |
| *Derive* | To obtain or get something from a source |
| *Sustenance* | Nourishment that supports life |
| *Apprehension* | The power or ability to grasp the importance, significance or meaning of something |
| *Enshrines* | Cherishes as sacred; encloses |

## 25. To Teach the Cause Is the Ultimate Purpose

In 1934 the government of Iran took several measures against the Bahá'ís throughout the country; towards the end of that year, Shoghi Effendi wrote this to an individual:

> I am so glad to note a decided improvement in the administrative conduct of Bahá'í affairs in India, and I trust and pray that the teaching work will as a result receive a fresh and unprecedented impetus. To teach the Cause is the ultimate purpose and the supreme objective of all Bahá'í institutions. These are but means to an end. May the Beloved grant you strength to enhance the splendid work you have already achieved.
>
> *(3 November 1934, DND 189-190)*

| | |
|---|---|
| *Unprecedented* | Having no earlier example or equivalent |
| *Impetus* | The energy or motivation to accomplish or undertake something |
| *Grant* | Allow something as favor |
| *Enhance* | To improve or add to the strength, worth, beauty or other desirable quality of something |
| *Splendid* | Impressive because of quality or size |

## 26. Be Lovers of Mankind

**In 1936,** a month before Shoghi Effendi wrote this to the Bahá'ís of the West, Martha Root met with Queen Marie of Romania for the eighth and last time:

> The Faith of Bahá'u'lláh has assimilated, by virtue of its creative, its regulative and ennobling energies, the varied races, nationalities, creeds and classes that have sought its shadow, and have pledged unswerving fealty to its cause. It has changed the hearts of its adherents, burned away their prejudices, stilled their passions, exalted their conceptions, ennobled their motives, coordinated their efforts, and transformed their outlook. While preserving their patriotism and safeguarding their lesser loyalties, it has made them lovers of mankind, and the determined upholders of its best and truest interests. While maintaining intact their belief in the Divine origin of their respective religions, it has enabled them to visualize the underlying purpose of these religions, to discover their merits, to recognize their sequence, their interdependence, their wholeness and unity, and to acknowledge the bond that vitally links them to itself. This universal, this transcending love which the followers of the Bahá'í Faith feel for their fellow-men, of whatever race, creed, class or nation, is neither mysterious nor can it be said to have been artificially stimulated. It is both spontaneous and genuine. They whose hearts are warmed by the energizing influence of God's creative love cherish His creatures for His sake, and recognize in every human face a sign of His reflected glory.
>
> Of such men and women it may be truly said that to them "every foreign land is a fatherland, and every fatherland a foreign land." For their citizenship, it must be remembered, is in the Kingdom of Bahá'u'lláh. Though willing to share to the utmost the temporal benefits and the fleeting joys which this earthly life can confer, though eager to participate in whatever activity that conduces to the richness, the happiness and peace of that life, they can, at no time, forget that it constitutes no more than a transient, a very brief stage of their existence, that they who live it are but pilgrims and wayfarers whose goal is the Celestial City, and whose home the Country of never-failing joy and brightness.
>
> *(11 March 1936, WOB 197-198)*

| | |
|---|---|
| *Assimilated* | Integrate somebody into a larger group, so that differences are minimized or eliminated, or become integrated in this way |
| *Unswerving* | Firm and unchanging in intent or purpose |

| | |
|---|---|
| *Fealty* | Loyalty or allegiance shown to someone |
| *Adherents* | Supporters |
| *Intact* | Not having any missing parts |
| *Temporal* | Lasting only for a time; passing |

## 27. Concentrate Our Energies on the Teaching Work

**Two** months before Shoghi Effendi wrote this letter in 1938 to the National Spiritual Assembly of the British Isles, the first Bahá'í of the British Isles, Mary Virginia Thornburgh Cropper, passed away in Kensington, London, and one month later Munírih Khanum, the Holy Mother, wife of 'Abdu'l-Bahá, passed away. Shoghi Effendi interred her body just west of the Shrine of Bahíyyih Khanum and erected a simple monument over her grave.

> I greatly welcome the determination of the English believers to concentrate their energies on the teaching work, and I pray from all my heart for the success of their high endeavours in this all-important field of Bahá'í service. Individuals as well as local Assemblies must arise and co-operate and persevere and refuse to allow any obstacle, however formidable, to dim their hopes or to deflect them from the course they have so spontaneously chosen to pursue. Kindly assure them of my constant prayers for their success.
>
> *(17 May 1938, UD 120)*

*Formidable* — Difficult to deal with or overcome
*Deflect* — Direct attention away

## 28. Empower the Bahá'í Youth

At the end of 1938, just a few months before World War II began with Britain and France declaring war on Germany after Germany invaded Poland, Shoghi Effendi addressed the Bahá'í youth of the United States and Canada:

> To the Bahá'í youth of America, moreover, I feel a word should be addressed in particular, as I survey the possibilities which a campaign of such gigantic proportions has to offer to the eager and enterprising spirit that so powerfully animates them in the service of the Cause of Bahá'u'lláh. Though lacking in experience and faced with insufficient resources, yet the adventurous spirit which they possess, and the vigor, the alertness, and optimism they have thus far so consistently shown, qualify them to play an active part in arousing the interest, and in securing the allegiance, of their fellow youth in those countries. No greater demonstration can be given to the peoples of both continents of the youthful vitality and the vibrant power animating the life, and the institutions of the nascent Faith of Bahá'u'lláh than an intelligent, persistent, and effective participation of the Bahá'í youth, of every race, nationality, and class, in both the teaching and administrative spheres of Bahá'í activity. Through such a participation the critics and enemies of the Faith, watching with varying degrees of skepticism and resentment, the evolutionary processes of the Cause of God and its institutions, can best be convinced of the indubitable truth that such a Cause is intensely alive, is sound to its very core, and its destinies in safe keeping. I hope, and indeed pray, that such a participation may not only redound to the glory, the power, and the prestige of the Faith, but may also react so powerfully on the spiritual lives, and galvanize to such an extent the energies of the youthful members of the Bahá'í community, as to empower them to display, in a fuller measure, their inherent capacities, and to unfold a further stage in their spiritual evolution under the shadow of the Faith of Bahá'u'lláh.
>
> *(25 December 1938, ADJ 58)*

| | |
|---|---|
| *Animates* | Rouses or inspires somebody to take action |
| *Insufficient* | Not enough |
| *Nascent* | Emerging; coming into existence |
| *Persistent* | Continuing despite problems |
| *Skepticism* | Doubting attitude |
| *Resentment* | Ill feeling |
| *Indubitable* | Not to be doubted |
| *Redound* | Contribute; have an effect |
| *Galvanize* | Arouse to awareness or action (see also next quote) |

## 29. Be Ambassadors of the Message of Bahá'u'lláh

Just two months before Martha Root, "foremost Hand raised by Bahá'u'lláh", died in Honolulu in September 1939, Shoghi Effendi wrote this to the American National Spiritual Assembly:

> Let the privileged few, the ambassadors of the Message of Bahá'u'lláh, bear in mind His words as they go forth on their errands of service to His Cause. "It behoveth whosoever willeth to journey for the sake of God, and whose intention is to proclaim His Word and quicken the dead, to bathe himself with the waters of detachment, and to adorn his temple with the ornaments of resignation and submission. Let trust in God be his shield, and reliance on God his provision, and the fear of God his raiment. Let patience be his helper, and praise-worthy conduct his succorer, and goodly deeds his army. Then will the concourse on high sustain him. Then will the denizens of the Kingdom of Names march forth with him, and the banners of Divine guidance and inspiration be unfurled on his right hand and before him."
>
> Faced with such a challenge, a community that has scaled thus far such peaks of enduring achievements can neither falter nor recoil. Confident in its destiny, reliant on its God-given power, fortified by the consciousness of its past victories, galvanized into action at the sight of a slowly disrupting civilization, it will - I can have no doubt - continue to fulfil unflinchingly the immediate requirements of its task, assured that with every step it takes and with each stage it traverses, a fresh revelation of Divine light and strength will guide and propel it forward until it consummates, in the fulness of time and in the plenitude of its power, the Plan inseparably bound up with its shining destiny.
>
> *(4 July 1939, MA 48)*

| | |
|---|---|
| *Resignation* | Accepting something with patience, especially with tolerance when it is unpleasant or unwelcome |
| *Submission* | The condition of being submissive, humble or compliant |
| *Succorer* | Something providing help or relief to somebody in a difficult situation |
| *Denizens* | Residents |
| *Unfurled* | Be rolled out or spread |
| *Scaled* | Climbed up something, especially a steep incline |
| *Enduring* | Persisting or surviving in the face of difficulties |
| *Falter* | To become unsure and hesitant |

| | |
|---|---|
| *Recoil* | To move back suddenly and violently, e.g. after an impact |
| *Fortified* | Made stronger |
| *Galvanized* | To react as if stimulated by an electric shock (see also last quote) |
| *Disrupting* | Destroying the order or orderly progression of something |
| *Unflinchingly* | Unhesitatingly; strongly |
| *Traverses* | Crosses; passes through something |
| *Consummates* | Achieves or fulfills something |
| *In the fulness of time* | After a period of time that must pass before something happens |
| *Plenitude* | The condition of being full, ample or complete |
| *Inseparably* | So closely linked as to be impossible to consider separately |

## 30. Extend Our Range of Activities

**In 1942**, the House of the Báb in Shiraz was attacked and damaged by fire and Lidia Zamenhof was killed in the gas chambers at Treblinka. At this time, Shoghi Effendi wrote to the British Isles:

> The steady progress and extension of Bahá'í activities in the British Isles is, no doubt, the direct consequence of the unswerving loyalty, the high courage, the incorruptible spirit and the exemplary devotion and steadfastness of the British believers, who have, simply and strikingly, demonstrated the quality of their faith and the soundness of their institutions in these days of unprecedented commotion, stress and peril. I feel proud of their record of service and of the evidence of their noble faith. The Beloved watches over them from the Abhá Kingdom. The Concourse on High extols their achievements and will reinforce their endeavours. They should confidently, gratefully, joyously and unitedly redouble their efforts, extend the range of their activities, rededicate themselves to their historic task and anticipate a renewed outpouring of Bahá'u'lláh's promised blessings and favours.
>
> *(20 June 1942, UD 153)*

| | |
|---|---|
| *Unswerving* | Firm and unchanging in intent or purpose |
| *Incorruptible* | Incapable of being morally corrupted, especially incapable of being bribed or motivated by selfish or base interests |
| *Strikingly* | Impressively |
| *Soundness* | Based on good sense; free from moral defects |
| *Extols* | Praises somebody or something with great enthusiasm and admiration |

## 31. The Magnet That Will Attract the Promised Blessings

LATER in 1942, when Shoghi Effendi asked Sutherland Maxwell to design the superstructure of the Shrine of the Báb, he wrote to the National Spiritual Assembly of India:

The pioneer activities in which the friends in India are so steadfastly, so energetically and so devotedly engaged, in spite of the perils, the uncertainties and the stress of the present hour, are a marvellous evidence of the indomitable spirit that animates them in the service of the Cause of Bahá'u'lláh. Perseverance is the magnet that will, in these days, attract the promised blessings of the Almighty Author of our beloved Faith. Unity and harmony constitute the basis on which the structure of these activities can securely rest. Self-sacrifice, audacity, undeviating adherence to the essentials of the Faith, will reinforce that structure and accelerate its rise. That the dear friends in India are increasingly demonstrating the quality and depth of their faith and the character and range of their accomplishments is a source of intense satisfaction to me, and I will continue to supplicate our Beloved to guide their steps, cheer their hearts, illumine their understanding, and fulfil their highest and noblest aspirations. He indeed is well pleased with the record of their past services, and will, if they redouble their efforts, enable them to achieve a signal victory.

(27 June 1942, DND 99)

| | |
|---|---|
| *Marvellous* | Something that inspires awe, amazement or admiration |
| *Indomitable* | Brave, determined, incapable of being overcome |
| *Animates* | Arouses someone into activity or motion |
| *Perseverance* | Steady and continued action, usually over a long period and especially despite difficulties or setbacks |
| *Constitute* | Make up the whole or a particular part of something |
| *Audacity* | Daring or willingness to challenge assumptions or conventions; tackling something difficult or dangerous |
| *Undeviating* | Not turning or changing, especially remaining constant or true to somebody or something |
| *Adherence* | To hold firmly to a belief, idea or opinion |

| | |
|---|---|
| *Reinforce* | To make something stronger by providing additional external support or internal stiffening for it |
| *Accelerate* | To cause to develop more quickly |

## 32. We Owe a Debt of Gratitude That No One Can Describe

**In 1944,** one month before the Centenary of the Declaration of the Báb when Shoghi Effendi unveiled the model of the Shrine of the Báb in Haifa, he wrote these moving words to the American Bahá'í community:

> To the band of pioneers, whether settlers or itinerant teachers, who have forsaken their homes, who have scattered far and wide, who have willingly sacrificed their comfort, their health and even their lives for the prosecution of this Plan; to the several committees and their auxiliary agencies that have been entrusted with special and direct responsibility for its efficient and orderly development and who have discharged their high responsibilities with exemplary vigor, courage and fidelity; to the national representatives of the community itself, who have vigilantly and tirelessly supervised, directed and coordinated the unfolding processes of this vast undertaking ever since its inception; to all those who, though not in the forefront of battle, have through their financial assistance and through the instrumentality of their deputies, contributed to the expansion and consolidation of the Plan, I myself, as well as the entire Bahá'í world, owe a debt of gratitude that no one can measure or describe. To the sacrifices they have made, to the courage they have so consistently shown, to the fidelity they have so remarkably displayed, to the resourcefulness, the discipline, the constancy and devotion they have so abundantly demonstrated, future generations viewing the magnitude of their labors in their proper perspective, will no doubt pay adequate tribute - a tribute no less ardent and well-deserved than the recognition extended by the present-day builders of the World Order of Bahá'u'lláh to the Dawn-Breakers, whose shining deeds have signalized the birth of the Heroic Age of His Faith.
>
> *(15 April 1944, MA 104-105)*

| | |
|---|---|
| *Itinerant* | Traveling from place to place |
| *Forsaken* | Given up, renounced or sacrificed something that gives pleasure |
| *Prosecution* | Carrying out of an activity until the very end |
| *Discharged* | Completed a duty, responsibility or promise successfully |
| *Vigor* | Intensity or forcefulness in the way something is done |
| *Fidelity* | Loyalty to an allegiance, promise or vow |

| | |
|---|---|
| *Vigilantly* | With alert watchfulness, especially to guard against danger, difficulties or errors |
| *Inception* | The beginning of something |
| *Instrumentality* | Serving as a crucial means, agent or tool |
| *Deputies* | Somebody fully authorized or appointed to act on behalf of somebody else |
| *Consistently* | Able to maintain a particular standard; reliably |
| *Abundantly* | Providing a more than plentiful supply of something |
| *Magnitude* | Greatness of size, volume or extent |
| *Ardent* | Feeling great passion, or felt very passionately |

## 33. What Must Have Precedence over All Other Considerations

In 1945, the war in Europe ended in May. The war in Japan ended in September, a month after Shoghi Effendi wrote this to Australia and New Zealand, and the United Nations was formally established in October:

> It is my fervent hope and prayer that the members of the Bahá'í communities of Australia and New Zealand, will, now that the machinery of the Administrative Order of their Faith has been erected, redouble their efforts to proclaim, with one voice and in a most effective manner, those vital and healing principles for which the great mass of their war-weary and much tested countrymen are hungering. This supreme issue must have precedence over all other considerations, must be given immediate and anxious attention, must be faced courageously and continually, and be regarded by individual believers as well as their elected representatives as the supreme objective of the manifold administrative institutions they have reared and are still labouring to establish. Complete harmony, mutual understanding, unity of purpose, coordination of efforts, prayerful consideration of, and mature deliberation on, all the aspects and requirements of this great and sacred objective can alone ensure its triumphant consummation during these years of stress and peril through which mankind is passing. May the national elected representatives of both communities set a superb example to their fellow-workers throughout that far-off continent, and enable them to win memorable victories in the service of their glorious Faith and its God-given institutions.
>
> *(8 August 1945, LAN 58-59)*

| | |
|---|---|
| *Supreme* | Greater than or superior to any other, especially above all others in power, authority, rank and status |
| *Precedence* | Priority; the right or need to be dealt with before somebody or something else |
| *Anxious* | Wanting to do something very much |
| *Manifold* | Many and various |
| *Reared* | Brought to maturity or self-sufficiency, usually through nurturing |
| *Ensure* | To make something certain |

| | |
|---|---|
| *Consummation* | The bringing of something to a satisfying conclusion; the final satisfying completion or achievement of something |
| *Superb* | Excellent |
| *Memorable* | Worth remembering |

## 34. The Universal Recognition of the Cause

During 1946, the restoration of the House of Bahá'u'lláh in Tihrán was completed; the National Spiritual Assembly of Germany and Austria was established in April; during the same month Shoghi Effendi instructed Sutherland Maxwell to set plans in motion for the first stages of the building of the superstructure of the Shrine of the Báb; the Second Seven Year Plan of the United States and Canada was launched, marking the beginning of the second epoch of the Formative Age. Later this year Shoghi Effendi wrote to the British Isles:

> The evidences of intensified activity and of notable progress on the part of the English believers in recent months have rejoiced my heart and deepened my feelings of admiration and gratitude for the manner in which they are discharging, individually and collectively, their high responsibilities. I long to hear of the steady progress of their Plan, and will continue to pray for the removal of every obstacle in their path. However considerable their recent achievements, they are still in the initial stage of their great unfolding mission, and are not even capable as yet of visualizing the possibilities or of estimating the consequences of their present-day labors. The consummation of their present task will mark the opening of a new era in the development of their community and will signalize the inauguration of a great epoch in the history of the Faith in their land—an epoch that must witness the universal recognition of their Cause and the proclamation of its truths, its claims and tenets, to the masses of their countrymen throughout the British Isles. The Plan they are now prosecuting will provide the machinery and establish the basic structure that will enable them to arouse the people, among all sections of the population, and aid them, systematically and gradually, to recognise Bahá'u'lláh, and support the nascent institutions of this World Order. Now it is their duty to lay an unassailable foundation for the great work that is to be undertaken in the future. There is no time to lose. Theirs is a priceless opportunity and a great privilege. They must neither vacillate nor falter. They must determinedly persevere until their immediate and distant goals have been attained.
>
> *(12 October 1946, UD 191-192)*

| | |
|---|---|
| *Notable* | Significant, interesting or unusual enough to deserve attention or to be recorded |
| *Prosecuting* | Continuing to do something, usually until it is finished or accomplished |
| *Nascent* | In the process of emerging, being born or starting to develop |

| | |
|---|---|
| *Unassailable* | So sound or well established that it cannot be challenged or overtaken |
| *Vacillate* | To be indecisive or irresolute, changing between one opinion and another |
| *Falter* | To become unsure and hesitant |

## 35. We Must Distinguish Our Record of Stewardship

**In 1950,** a month before the Centenary of the Martyrdom of the Báb was commemorated, Shoghi Effendi expressed this to the National Spiritual Assembly of Canada:

> That this community will never relax in its high endeavours, that the vision of its glorious mission will not be suffered to be dimmed, that obstacles, however formidable, will neither dampen its zeal or deflect it from its purpose, is my confident hope and earnest prayer. He Who watches over its destinies, from Whose pen testimonies so significant and soul thrilling have flowed, will no doubt continue to direct its steps, to shower upon it His loving bounties, to surround it with His constant care, and to enable it to scale loftier heights on its ascent towards the summit of its destiny.
>
> With a heart brimful with gratitude for all that this community has so far achieved, and throbbing with hope for the future exploits that will distinguish its record of stewardship to the Faith of Bahá'u'lláh, I pray that by its acts, this community will prove itself worthy of the trust confided to its care, and the station to which it has been called.
>
> (23 June 1950, MC 18)

| | |
|---|---|
| *Formidable* | Difficult to deal with or overcome |
| *Dampen* | Make less strong or intense |
| *Zeal* | Great energy or enthusiasm for a cause or objective |
| *Deflect* | Direct attention away |
| *Scale* | Climb up or over (something high and steep) |
| *Loftier* | More exalted and refined |
| *Ascent* | To rise to a higher point, level, degree |
| *Summit* | Highest point |
| *Brimful* | Ready to overflow |
| *Throbbing* | Beating rapidly and forcefully |
| *Exploits* | Acts or deeds, especially brilliant or heroic ones |
| *Stewardship* | Someone's stewardship of something is the way in which that person controls or organizes it |

## 36. The Spiritual Potentialities That Will Empower Us

In the significant year 1951, Shoghi Effendi received the original manuscript of the Kitáb-i-Iqán in the handwriting of 'Abdu'l-Bahá with some marginal additions by Bahá'u'lláh, and placed it in the International Bahá'í Archives; in January, he announced the establishment of the International Bahá'í Council; and on the same day that he wrote this to the National Spiritual Assembly of Germany, he announced the completion of the restoration of the House of 'Abbúd:

> The record of service stretching behind them is indeed highly inspiring. The vision of future victories at home and in distant fields now unfolding before them is even more glorious and highly challenging. The more they consecrate themselves to their present tasks, the more faithfully and promptly they fulfil the requirements of the Plan to which they stand committed, the sooner will they acquire the spiritual potentialities that will empower them to qualify for the successful conduct and the ultimate consummation of so colossal an enterprise destined to shed so great and imperishable a lustre on both their community and nation.
>
> That they may be vouchsafed by Providence all the strength and guidance they require for the attainment of their immediate goal, that they may prove themselves worthy of receiving a still greater measure of celestial strength and Divine sustenance for the achievement of their ultimate objective is the dearest wish of my heart and constant prayer.
>
> *(2 March 1951, LDG Vol. I, 172)*

| | |
|---|---|
| *Consecrate*: | Dedicate to a sacred purpose |
| *Potentialities* | Capacities for growth and development |
| *Empower* | To give somebody a greater sense of confidence or self-esteem |
| *Colossal* | Very great or impressive |
| *Enterprise* | A new, often risky, venture that involves confidence and initiative |
| *Imperishable* | Not forgotten or ignored over time |
| *Lustre* | Glory or distinction |
| *Vouchsafed* | Given, granted or allowed |
| *Providence* | God's guidance |
| *Attainment* | The achievement of the goals that somebody has set |
| *Celestial* | Heavenly |
| *Sustenance* | Something that gives support, endurance or strength |

## 37. Let Us Place Our Share
## on the Altar of Sacrifice

**In January** 1954 Dorothy Baker, Hand of the Cause of God, died in a plane crash in the Mediterranean Sea near the island of Elba. When Marion Jack died the same year in Sofia, Bulgaria, Shoghi Effendi called her 'a shining example' to pioneers of present and future generations of East and West and wrote to the American Baháʹís:

> It is therefore imperative for the individual American believer, and particularly for the affluent, the independent, the comfort-loving and those obsessed by material pursuits, to step forward, and dedicate their resources, their time, their very lives to a Cause of such transcendence that no human eye can even dimly perceive its glory. Let them resolve, instantly and unhesitatingly, to place, each according to his circumstances, his share on the altar of Baháʹí sacrifice, lest, on a sudden, unforeseen calamities rob them of a considerable portion of the earthly things they have amassed.
>
> Now if ever is the time to tread the path which the dawn-breakers of a previous age have so magnificently trodden. Now is the time to carry out, in the spirit and in the letter, the fervent wish so pathetically voiced by ʻAbduʹl-Bahá, Who longed, as attested in the Tablets of the Divine Plan, to "travel though on foot and in the utmost poverty" and raise "in cities, villages, mountains, deserts and oceans" "the call of Yá-Baháʹuʹl-Abhá!"
>
> (28 July 1954, CF 131-132)

| | |
|---|---|
| *Imperative* | Absolutely necessary or unavoidable |
| *Affluent* | Having an abundance of material wealth |
| *Pursuits* | An occupation, career, interests |
| *Transcendence* | Supremity; going beyond known limits |
| *Resolve* | To come to a firm decision |
| *Considerable* | A great deal or amount |
| *Amassed* | Having brought together a large quantity of things over time |
| *Fervent* | Exhibiting or marked by great intensity of feeling |
| *Pathetically* | Marked by sorrow or melancholy |
| *Attested* | Affirmed to be true or genuine |

## 38. Our Concerted Exertions Must Be Adequate in Range and Quality

In 1957, one month after Shoghi Effendi added protection of the Cause to the duties of the Hands of the Cause, he wrote to the National Spiritual Assembly of the Benelux Countries:

> That they may prove themselves worthy of their high calling; that they may rise to such heights as to excite the unqualified admiration of their brethren not only in the European continent but throughout both the Eastern and Western Hemispheres; that they may, through the range and quality of their concerted exertions, draw forth a measure of Divine bounty adequate to meet the pressing needs and manifold requirements of their glorious Mission, is my ardent and constant prayer for them all as I lay my head on the threshold of His Most Holy Shrine.
>
> (5 July 1957, DC 152)

| | |
|---|---|
| *Unqualified* | Absolute |
| *Concerted* | Planned or accomplished together |
| *Manifold* | Many and various |
| *Ardent* | Passionate |

Photograph by Nayyirih G. de Koning-Tahzib

# Coping with Tests and Difficulties

> You gain strength, courage and confidence by every experience in which you really stop to look fear in the face. You are able to say to yourself, 'I have lived through this horror. I can take the next thing that comes along.' You must do the thing you think you cannot do.
>
> *Eleanor Roosevelt*
> *US diplomat & reformer (1884 - 1962)*

**We will** be faced with many tests and difficulties while we are serving the Faith. How to cope with and surmount these trying times is often very difficult, and they can be hard to bear. We find in Shoghi Effendi's letters advice and admonitions on how to overcome what comes in our path and be resilient.

## 39. Severe Mental Tests Will Sweep over the West

**In 1923,** Amelia Collins contributed the funds necessary to complete the Western Pilgrim House; Shoghi Effendi sent his early translation of the "Hidden Words" to America; the keys to the Shrine of Bahá'u'lláh were returned to Shoghi Effendi; and Shoghi Effendi wrote to Bahá'ís in America, Great Britain, Germany, France, Switzerland, Italy, Japan and Australasia about Bahá'í administration, outlining the process for annual elections of assemblies and calling for the establishment of local and national funds. It was in this year that Shoghi Effendi returned to Haifa from Switzerland one month before he wrote this to the Bahá'ís of Australia and New Zealand:

> ... How often we seem to forget the clear and repeated warnings of our beloved Master, who in particular during the concluding years of his mission on earth, laid stress on the severe mental tests that would inevitably sweep over his loved ones of the West ... tests that would purge, purify and prepare them for their noble mission in life.
>
> And as to the world's evil plight, we need but recall the writings and sayings of Bahá'u'lláh, who, more than fifty years ago, declared in terms prophetic the prime cause of the ills and sufferings of mankind, and set forth their true and divine remedy. "Should the lamp of Religion be hidden", He declared, "chaos and confusion will ensue." How admirably fitting and applicable are these words to the present state of mankind!
>
> Ours then is the duty and privilege to labour, by day, by night, amidst the storm and stress of these troublous days, that we may quicken the zeal of our fellow-man, rekindle their hopes, stimulate their interests, open their eyes to the true Faith of God and enlist their active support in the carrying out of our common task for the peace and regeneration of the world.
>
> *(2 December 1923, LAN 1-2)*

| | |
|---|---|
| *Purge* | Make somebody pure and free from guilt, sin or defilement |
| *Plight* | A difficult or dangerous situation, especially a sad or desperate predicament |
| *Amidst* | In the middle of: surrounded by |
| *Quicken* | To stimulate something such as interest or enthusiasm |
| *Zeal* | Energetic and unflagging enthusiasm, especially for a cause or idea |
| *Rekindle* | To revive or renew something such as a feeling or interest |

## 40. The Plight of Mankind

**In 1924,** Shoghi Effendi wrote this message to the Bahá'ís throughout America in between his return to Haifa and another departure for six months:

> The plight of mankind, the condition and circumstances under which we live and labor are truly disheartening, and the darkness of prejudice and ill-will enough to chill the stoutest heart. Disillusion and dismay are invading the hearts of peoples and nations, and the hope and vision of a united and regenerated humanity is growing dimmer and dimmer every day. Time-honored institutions, cherished ideals, and sacred traditions are suffering in these days of bewildering change, from the effects of the gravest onslaught, and the precious fruit of centuries of patient and earnest labor is faced with peril. Passions, supposed to have been curbed and subdued, are now burning fiercer than ever before, and the voice of peace and good-will seems drowned amid unceasing convulsions and turmoil. What, let us ask ourselves, should be our attitude as we stand under the all-seeing eye of our vigilant Master, gazing at a sad spectacle so utterly remote from the spirit which He breathed into the world? Are we to follow in the wake of the wayward and the despairing? Are we to allow our vision of so unique, so enduring, so precious a Cause to be clouded by the stain and dust of worldly happenings, which, no matter how glittering and far-reaching in their immediate effects, are but the fleeting shadows of an imperfect world? Are we to be carried away by the flood of hollow and conflicting ideas, or are we to stand, unsubdued and unblemished, upon the everlasting rock of God's Divine Instructions? Shall we not equip ourselves with a clear and full understanding of their purpose and implications for the age we live in, and with an unconquerable resolve arise to utilize them, intelligently and with scrupulous fidelity, for the enlightenment and the promotion of the good of all mankind?
>
> Humanity, torn with dissension and burning with hate, is crying at this hour for a fuller measure of that love which is born of God, that love which in the last resort will prove the one solvent of its incalculable difficulties and problems. Is it not incumbent upon us, whose hearts are aglow with love for Him, to make still greater effort, to manifest that love in all its purity and power in our dealings with our fellow-men? May our love of our beloved Master, so ardent, so disinterested in all its aspects, find its true expression in love for our fellow-brethren and sisters in the faith as well as for all mankind. I assure you, dear friends, that progress in such matters as these is limitless and infinite, and that upon the extent of our achievements along this line will ultimately depend the success of our mission in life.
>
> *(23 February 1924, BA 61-62)*

| | |
|---|---|
| *Plight* | A difficult or dangerous situation |
| *Disheartening* | Making somebody lose hope or enthusiasm |
| *Stoutest* | Possessing great courage and determination |
| *Disillusion* | Disappointment from discovering that something is not as good as one believed it to be |
| *Dismay* | A sudden loss of courage or confidence |
| *Regenerated* | Newborn |
| *Time-honored* | Respected or continued because of having been the custom for a long time |
| *Cherished* | Valued highly, especially something such as a right, freedom or privilege |
| *Gravest* | Involving serious consequences such as danger or harm |
| *Onslaught* | A powerful attack or force that overwhelms somebody or something |
| *Earnest* | Serious |
| *Peril* | Danger |
| *Curbed* | Controlled or limited, especiallly something that is not desirable |
| *Subdued* | Quieted, or brought under control |
| *Unceasing* | Never stopping |
| *Convulsions* | Uncontrollable shaking |
| *Turmoil* | Confused disturbance |
| *Vigilant* | Always being careful to notice things, especially possible danger |
| *Gazing* | Looking at something or someone for a long time, intently and with fixed attention |
| *Spectacle* | Some strange or remarkable sight, an unusual display |
| *Utterly* | In an extreme or complete way |
| *Remote* | Far away |
| *Wake* | If something happens in the wake of something else, it happens after it and often because of it |
| *Wayward* | Undisciplined or self-willed; headstrong, willful or rebellious |
| *Despairing* | Feeling or showing loss of hope |
| *Scrupulous* | Diligent and thorough |
| *Fidelity* | Continuing faithfulness to a person, cause or belief |
| *Dissension* | Disagreement or difference of opinion, especially when leading to open conflict |
| *Solvent* | Something that dissolves or can dissolve; also, something that solves or explains |
| *Incumbent* | Necessary as a result of a duty, responsibility or obligation |

## 41. Problems Will Gradually Be Solved

In 1933, the 50 Bahá'ís imprisoned in Adana, Turkey, were released. One month later, Shoghi Effendi wrote to Louise Drake Wright, a travel teacher to the Netherlands:

> The problems which confront the believers at the present time, whether social, spiritual, economic or administrative will be gradually solved as the number and the resources of the friends multiply and their capacity for service and for the application of Bahá'í principles develops. They should be patient, confident and active in utilizing every possible opportunity that presents itself within the limits now necessarily imposed upon them. May the Almighty aid them to fulfil their highest hopes.
>
> *(11 March 1933, DC 24)*

*Utilizing* — Making use of something
*Imposed* — Forced to be accepted, undertaken or complied with

## 42. Be Undismayed

**In April** of 1938, Munírih Khánum, the Holy Mother, wife of 'Abdu'l-Bahá, died. Shoghi Effendi interred her body just west of the Shrine of Bahíyyíh Khánum and erected a simple monument over her grave. In July, Queen Marie of Romania died. In that month, Shoghi Effendi wrote to the Bahá'ís of the United States and Canada:

> ... Whereas every apparent trial with which the able unfathomable wisdom of the Almighty deems it necessary to afflict His chosen community serves only to demonstrate afresh its essential solidarity and to consolidate its inward strength, each of the successive crises in the fortunes of a decadent age exposes more convincingly than the one preceding it the corrosive influences that are fast sapping the vitality and undermining the basis of its declining institutions.
>
> For such demonstrations of the interpositions of an ever-watchful Providence they who stand identified with the Community of the Most Great Name must feel eternally grateful. From every fresh token of His unfailing blessing on the one hand, and of His visitation on the other, they cannot but derive immense hope and courage. Alert to seize every opportunity which the revolutions of the wheel of destiny within their Faith offers them, and undismayed by the prospect of spasmodic convulsions that must sooner or later fatally affect those who have refused to embrace its light, they, and those who will labor after them, must press forward until the processes now set in motion will have each spent its force and contributed its share towards the birth of the Order now stirring in the womb of a travailing age.
>
> *(25 December 1938, ADJ 1-2)*

| | |
|---|---|
| *Unfathomable* | Impossible to measure or understand |
| *Deems* | Considers to be |
| *Afflict* | Cause distress |
| *Corrosive* | Gradually destructive |
| *Sapping* | Draining; weakening |
| *Interposition* | Coming between things to exert authority |
| *Spasmodic* | Irregular; intermittent |

## 43. The Promise

In 1938, persecution of the Bahá'ís of Iran continued throughout the country. Bahá'ís marrying without a Muslim ceremony were investigated, including several hundred in Tihrán alone. Most were imprisoned pending trial and were imprisoned for six to eight months afterwards and fined. Shoghi Effendi wrote this moving passage to the United States and Canada:

> Though the task be long and arduous, yet the prize which the All-Bountiful Bestower has chosen to confer upon you is of such preciousness that neither tongue nor pen can befittingly appraise it. Though the goal towards which you are now so strenuously striving be distant, and as yet undisclosed to men's eyes, yet its promise lies firmly embedded in the authoritative and unalterable utterances of Bahá'u'lláh. Though the course He has traced for you seems, at times, lost in the threatening shadows with which a stricken humanity is now enveloped, yet the unfailing light He has caused to shine continually upon you is of such brightness that no earthly dusk can ever eclipse its splendor. Though small in numbers, and circumscribed as yet in your experiences, powers, and resources, yet the Force which energizes your mission is limitless in its range and incalculable in its potency. Though the enemies which every acceleration in the progress of your mission must raise up be fierce, numerous, and unrelenting, yet the invisible Hosts which, if you persevere, must, as promised, rush forth to your aid, will, in the end, enable you to vanquish their hopes and annihilate their forces. Though the ultimate blessings that must crown the consummation of your mission be undoubted, and the Divine promises given you firm and irrevocable, yet the measure of the goodly reward which every one of you is to reap must depend on the extent to which your daily exertions will have contributed to the expansion of that mission and the hastening of its triumph.
>
> *(25 December 1938, ADJ 13)*

| | |
|---|---|
| *Arduous* | Difficult and trying |
| *Confer* | To give an honor |
| *Strenuously* | Requiring physical effort, energy, stamina or strength |
| *Embedded* | Set or fixed firmly and deeply |
| *Unalterable* | Not able to be changed |
| *Traced* | Laid out; planned |
| *Enveloped* | Enclosed or enfolded completely as if with a covering |

| | |
|---|---|
| *Dusk* | The period of the day after the sun has gone below the horizon but before the sky has become dark |
| *Eclipse* | To block the light falling on something, or cast a shadow on it |
| *Circumscribed* | To be limited |
| *Unrelenting* | Unyielding or unswerving in determination or resolve |
| *Vanquish* | To defeat an opponent |
| *Annihilate* | To destroy something completely, especially so that it ceases to exist |
| *Irrevocable* | Impossible to revoke, undo or change |
| *Reap* | To obtain something, especially as a consequence of previous effort or action |

## 44. Pursue the Present Plan

**Shoghi** Effendi outlined further the processes involved:

> ... Who knows but that these few remaining, fast-fleeting years, may not be pregnant with events of unimaginable magnitude, with ordeals more severe than any that humanity has as yet experienced, with conflicts more devastating than any which have preceded them. Dangers, however sinister, must, at no time, dim the radiance of their new-born faith. Strife and confusion, however bewildering, must never befog their vision. Tribulations, however afflictive, must never shatter their resolve. Denunciations, however clamorous, must never sap their loyalty. Upheavals, however cataclysmic, must never deflect their course. The present Plan, embodying the budding hopes of a departed Master, must be pursued, relentlessly pursued, whatever may befall them in the future, however distracting the crises that may agitate their country or the world. Far from yielding in their resolve, far from growing oblivious of their task, they should, at no time, however much buffeted by circumstances, forget that the synchronization of such world-shaking crises with the progressive unfoldment and fruition of their divinely appointed task is itself the work of Providence, the design of an inscrutable Wisdom, and the purpose of an all-compelling Will, a Will that directs and controls, in its own mysterious way, both the fortunes of the Faith and the destinies of men. Such simultaneous processes of rise and of fall, of integration and of disintegration, of order and chaos, with their continuous and reciprocal reactions on each other, are but aspects of a greater Plan, one and indivisible, whose Source is God, whose author is Bahá'u'lláh, the theater of whose operations is the entire planet, and whose ultimate objectives are the unity of the human race and the peace of all mankind.
>
> (25 December 1938, ADJ 60-61)

| | |
|---|---|
| *Magnitude* | Greatness of extent or importance |
| *Devastating* | Damaging; very upsetting |
| *Sinister* | Suggesting evil |
| *Clamorous* | Making loud demands or complaints |
| *Cataclysmic* | Causing great destruction |
| *Relentlessly* | Ceaselessly and intensely |
| *Oblivious* | Forgetful |
| *Buffeted* | Struck repeatedly and violently; battered |
| *Synchronization* | Happening together |
| *Inscrutable* | Hard to interpret |
| *Reciprocal* | Felt by both sides of a situation |

## 45. Be Not Afraid of Any Criticism

**Shoghi** Effendi gives insight on how to cope during difficult times:

> Let not, however, the invincible army of Bahá'u'lláh, who in the West, and at one of its potential storm centers is to fight, in His name and for His sake, one of its fiercest and most glorious battles, be afraid of any criticism that might be directed against it. Let it not be deterred by any condemnation with which the tongue of the slanderer may seek to debase its motives. Let it not recoil before the threatening advance of the forces of fanaticism, of orthodoxy, of corruption, and of prejudice that may be leagued against it. The voice of criticism is a voice that indirectly reinforces the proclamation of its Cause. Unpopularity but serves to throw into greater relief the contrast between it and its adversaries, while ostracism is itself the magnetic power that must eventually win over to its camp the most vociferous and inveterate amongst its foes. Already in the land where the greatest battles of the Faith have been fought, and its most rapacious enemies have lived, the march of events, the slow yet steady infiltration of its ideals, and the fulfillment of its prophecies, have resulted not only in disarming and in transforming the character of some of its most redoubtable enemies, but also in securing their firm and unreserved allegiance to its Founders. So complete a transformation, so startling a reversal of attitude, can only be effected if that chosen vehicle which is designed to carry the Message of Bahá'u'lláh to the hungry, the restless, and unshepherded multitudes is itself thoroughly cleansed from the defilements which it seeks to remove.
>
> *(25 December 1938, ADJ 42-43)*

| | |
|---|---|
| *Invincible* | Unconquerable, indestructible |
| *Deterred* | Prevented from acting, as by fear or doubt |
| *Condemnation* | Stating that somebody is some way wrong or unacceptable |
| *Slanderer* | Someone who makes false and malicious statements |
| *Debase* | To reduce somebody in status, significance, or moral worth |
| *Recoil* | To shrink back, as in fear or repugnance |
| *Ostracism* | Banishing or excluding somebody from society or from a particular group, either formally or informally |
| *Vociferous* | Shouting in a noisy and determined way |
| *Inveterate* | Firmly established and of long standing |

| | |
|---|---|
| *Rapacious* | Engaging in violent pillaging and likely to harm or destroy things |
| *Redoubtable* | Having personal qualities worthy of respect or fear |
| *Defilements* | Things that pollute, corrupt, or damage a reputation |

## 46. No Sacrifice Can Be Regarded As Too Great

In May of 1940, Shoghi Effendi and Rúhíyyih Khanum left Haifa for Italy en route to London. After obtaining a visa for Britain in Rome, they left for England via France. A few days later the Italians entered the war against the Allies. In June they left Paris for England one day before the city was occupied by the Nazis. In July they left England for South Africa. This was the only route open back to Palestine, as Italy's entrance into the war had closed the Mediterranean to Allied ships. The trip across Africa took them to Stanleyville, Congo, Juba in the Sudan; down the Nile to Khartoum and back to Palestine through Cairo. Less than two weeks before they were back in Haifa, Shoghi Effendi wrote this to The National Assembly of India:

> I wish to reassure you in person of my fervent and continued prayers for the protection, the success and the spiritual advancement of the community of the Indian and Burmese believers who, under your direction, and stimulated by the initiative and example, of their national elected representatives, are arising, in these days of widespread confusion, turmoil and danger, to carry out the Plan they are pledged to fulfill. No sacrifice can be regarded as too great for the attainment of so great and splendid an objective. They should persevere in their task, undaunted by the rising tide of calamity and despair which afflicts the world, and which is mysteriously paving the way for its unification and ultimate redemption. May the Beloved guide every step you take, and bless every endeavour you exert in His path.
>
> *(14 December 1940, DND 87-88)*

| | |
|---|---|
| *Undaunted* | Courageously resolute, especially in the face of danger or difficulty; not discouraged |
| *Paving* | Creating the circumstances to enable (something) to happen |
| *Ultimate* | Coming or attained at the end of a series of stages, and often constituting the completion of something |
| *Redemption* | A thing that saves someone from error or evil |
| *Exert* | To attempt to have a powerful effect on a situation |

## 47. Face the Trials of the Present Hour

In 1941 nine Bahá'ís were arrested in Sangsar, Khurásán, Iran, and banished to other towns for closing their shops on Bahá'í holy days; and John Henry Dunn, Hand of the Cause of God, died in Sydney. It was in that year that Shoghi Effendi wrote this to the American believers:

> As opposition to the Faith, from whatever source it may spring, whatever form it may assume, however violent its outbursts, is admittedly the motive-power that galvanizes on the one hand, the souls of its valiant defenders, and taps for them, on the other, fresh springs of that Divine and inexhaustible Energy, we who are called upon to represent, defend and promote its interests, should, far from regarding any manifestation of hostility as an evidence of the weakening of the pillars of the Faith, acclaim it as both a God-sent gift and a God-sent opportunity which, if we remain undaunted, we can utilize for the furtherance of His Faith and the routing and complete elimination of its adversaries.
>
> The Heroic Age of the Faith, born in anguish, nursed in adversity, and terminating in trials as woeful as those that greeted its birth, has been succeeded by that Formative Period which is to witness the gradual crystallization of those creative energies which the Faith has released, and the consequent emergence of that World Order for which those forces were made to operate.
>
> Fierce and relentless will be the opposition which this crystallization and emergence must provoke. The alarm it must and will awaken, the envy it will certainly arouse, the misrepresentations to which it will remorselessly be subjected, the setbacks it must, sooner or later, sustain, the commotions to which it must eventually give rise, the fruits it must in the end garner, the blessings it must inevitably bestow and the glorious, the Golden Age, it must irresistibly usher in, are just beginning to be faintly perceived, and will, as the old order crumbles beneath the weight of so stupendous a Revelation, become increasingly apparent and arresting.
>
> Not ours to attempt to survey the distant scene; ours rather the duty to face the trials of the present hour, to ponder its meaning, to discharge its obligations, to meet its challenge and utilize the opportunity it offers to the fullest extent of our ability and power.
>
> *(12 August 1941, MA 79)*

| | |
|---|---|
| *Undaunted* | Not afraid or stopped by the prospect of defeat, loss or failure |
| *Routing* | A severe and humiliating defeat |
| *Anguish* | Extreme anxiety or emotional torment |
| *Woeful* | Bringing or causing great distress or sorrow |
| *Relentless* | Ceaseless and intense |
| *Remorselessly* | Continuing without lessening in strength or intensity |
| *Garner* | To earn or acquire something by effort |
| *Usher in* | To guide, to lead |
| *Ponder* | Think about seriously before making a conclusion |

## 48. Adversity Prepares the Hearts of Men

Two months befoe Shoghi Effendi wrote the following to the National Spiritual Assembly of India in December 1941, Ridá Sháh in Iran abdicated and Muhammad-Ridá Sháh acceded to the throne:

> The news conveyed by your latest communication has rejoiced my heart. The manner in which the friends have arisen to promote the teaching work throughout their country merits the highest praise. By their enthusiasm, their self-abnegation, the determination and vigour they display, they have lent a fresh impetus to the onward march of the Faith and the expansion of its institutions and the multiplication of its administrative centres. The perils of the present hour, the repercussions of this tremendous world ordeal on their native land, must, in no wise, alarm or discourage them. Their purpose must never be deflected, their enthusiasm never dimmed, their vision never obscured, their exertions never discontinued. Adversity prepares the hearts of men, and paves the way for a wholehearted and general acceptance of the tenets and claims of our beloved Faith. Challenged by the obstacles in their path, encouraged by work already initiated, assured of the Divine Promise of Bahá'u'lláh, let them forge ahead until their goal is attained.
>
> My prayers will ever surround them.
>
> *(27 December 1941, DND 95-96)*

| | |
|---|---|
| *Self-abnegation* | The setting aside of self-interest for the sake of others or for a belief or principle |
| *Paves* | Prepares a smooth easy way |
| *Tenets* | Beliefs, convictions, teachings |
| *Forge* | To advance gradually but steadily |

## 49. Arise Without Fear

**Some** months after Shoghi Effendi's book God Passes By was published in 1945, he wrote to the American Bahá'í Community:

> There is no time to lose. The hour is ripe for the proclamation, without fear, without reserve, and without hesitation, and on a scale never as yet undertaken, of the One Message that can alone extricate humanity from the morass into which it is steadily sinking, and from which they who claim to be the followers of the Most Great Name can and will eventually rescue it. The sooner they who labor for the recognition and triumph of His Faith in the new world arise to carry out these inescapable duties, the sooner will the hopes, the aims and objectives of 'Abdu'l-Bahá as enshrined in His own Plan, be translated from the realm of vision to the plane of actuality and manifest the full force of the potentialities with which they have been endued.
>
> *(29 March 1945, MA 118)*

| | |
|---|---|
| *Extricate* | To release somebody or something with difficulty from a physical constraint or an unpleasant or complicated situation |
| *Morass* | A frustrating, confusing or unmanageable situation that makes any kind of progress extremely slow |
| *Enshrined* | Preserved or cherished as sacred |
| *Realm* | An area or domain, e.g. of thought or knowledge |

## 50. So Much Depends Upon Us

In 1946 the restoration of the House of Bahá'u'lláh in Tihrán was completed; in April Shoghi Effendi instructed Sutherland Maxwell to set plans in motion for the first stages of the building of the superstructure of the Shrine of the Báb; the Second Seven Year Plan of the United States and Canada was launched, marking the beginning of the second epoch of the Formative Age. Shoghi Effendi wrote this to the American Bahá'ís:

> It is not for us, at this crucial hour, to delve into the future, to speculate on the possibilities of the Plan and its orientation, to conjecture on its impact on the unfoldment of an embryonic World Order, or to dwell on the glories and triumphs which it may hold in store, or to seek to delineate the mysterious course which a God given Mission, impelled by forces beyond our power to predict or appraise, may pursue. To try to obtain a clear view of the shape of things to come would be premature inasmuch as the glittering prizes to be won are directly dependent on the measure of success which the combined efforts that are now being exerted must yield. Ours is the duty to fix our gaze with undeviating attention on the duties and responsibilities confronting us at this present hour, to concentrate our resources, both material and spiritual, on the tasks that lie immediately ahead, to insure that no time is wasted, that no opportunity is missed, that no obligation is evaded, that no task is half-heartedly performed, that no decision is procrastinated. The task summoning us to a challenge, unprecedented in its gravity and force, is too vast and sacred, the time too short, the hour too perilous, the workers too few, the call too insistent, the resources too inadequate, for us to allow these precious and fleeting hours to slip from our grasp, and to suffer the prizes within our reach to be endangered or forfeited. So much depends upon us, so pregnant with possibilities is the present stage in the evolution of the Plan, that great and small, individuals, groups and Assemblies, white and colored, young and old, neophytes and veterans, settlers, pioneers, itinerant teachers and administrators, as isolated believers, as organizers of groups, and as contributors to the formation of local or national Assemblies, as builders of the Temple, as laborers on the home teaching front, or in Latin America, or in the new transatlantic field of service - all, without exception and in every sphere of activity, however modest, restricted, or inconspicuous, must participate and labor, assiduously and continually, until every ounce of our energy is spent, until, tired but blissful, our promised harvest is brought in, and our pledge to our Beloved fully redeemed.

*(15 June 1946, MA 143-144)*

| | |
|---|---|
| *Delve into* | To investigate or research something thoroughly in order to obtain information |
| *Conjecture* | To make judgments or opinions on the basis of incomplete or inconclusive information; to guess |
| *Delineate* | To describe or explain something in detail |
| *Appraise* | To evaluate the worth, significance or status of something |
| *Undeviating* | Not turning or changing; remaining constant or true to something |
| *Gravity* | The seriousness of something considered in terms of its unfavorable consequences |
| *Forfeited* | To be deprived of, to be lost |
| *Neophytes* | Beginners |
| *Itinerant* | Traveling from place to place |
| *Inconspicuous* | Not obvious |
| *Assiduously* | Showing persistent and hard working effort in doing something |

## 51. Trials and Disappointments May Tax Our Patience

**Several** months after the launching of the Second Seven Year Plan of the United States and Canada, Shoghi Effendi wrote this to the American Bahá'í Community:

> The sterner the task, the graver the responsibilities, the wider the field of exertion, the more persistently must the privileged members of this enviable community strive, and the loftier must be the height to which they should aspire, in the course of their God-given mission, and throughout every stage in the irresistible and divinely guided evolution of their community life.
>
> Setbacks may well surprise them; trials and disappointments may tax their patience and resourcefulness; the forces of darkness, either from within or from without, may seek to dampen their ardor, to disrupt their unity and break their spirit; pitfalls may surround the little band that must act as a vanguard to the host which must, in the years to come, spiritually raise up the sorely ravaged continent of Europe. None of these, however fierce, sinister or unyielding they may appear, must be allowed to deflect the protagonists of a God-impelled Plan, from the course which 'Abdu'l-Bahá has chosen for them, and which the agencies of a firmly established, laboriously erected, Administrative Order, are now enabling them to effectively pursue.
>
> That they may press forward with undiminished fervor, with undimmed vision, with unfaltering steps, with indivisible unity, with unflinching determination until the shining goal is attained is my constant prayer, my ardent hope, and the dearest wish of my heart.
>
> *(20 July 1946, MA 146-147)*

| | |
|---|---|
| *Sterner* | More rigid, strict and uncompromising |
| *Graver* | Requiring serious thought; more momentous |
| *Enviable* | So desirable that other people feel envy |
| *Loftier* | Of a higher rank or status |
| *Aspire* | To seek to attain a goal |
| *Setbacks* | Things that reverse or delay your progress |
| *Tax* | To strain or make a heavy demand |
| *Ardor* | Strong feeling; enthusiasm; devotion |
| *Disrupt* | To break apart |
| *Pitfalls* | Potential and usually unanticipated disasters or difficulties |
| *Vanguard* | Leading position or people |
| *Ravaged* | Badly damaged; devastated |

| | |
|---|---|
| *Sinister* | Suggesting or threatening evil |
| *Deflect* | Direct attention away |
| *Protagonists* | Supporters |
| *Undiminished* | Not reduced or lessened |
| *Fervor* | Extremely passionate enthusiasm |
| *Unflinching* | Strong and unhesitating |

## 52. We Must Encounter Critical Stages with Unswerving Resolution

The Haziratu'l-Quds of Tihrán was completed; the National Spiritual Assembly of India and Burma was established; the National Spiritual Assembly of the United States and Canada was accredited by the United Nations as a non-governmental organization in the beginning half of 1947 before Shoghi Effendi wrote this appendage to the National Spiritual Assembly of the British Isles:

> A staggering responsibility rests on the shoulders of those who have been called upon to assist in the operation of the initial stages of this heroic colossal enterprise, and to participate in the privilege of directing its course, and nursing its infant strength. Setbacks and reverses are inevitable as this mighty Plan progresses and expands. Critical stages in its unfoldment must be encountered with unswerving resolution and confident hope. Whatever hardships and sacrifices its future prosecution may involve must be borne with courage, pride and thankfulness. To insure its speedy advancement every issue must be subordinated to its vital requirements, and every individual effort co-ordinated with the agencies designed for its execution.
>
> *(24 October 1947, UD 208)*

| | |
|---|---|
| *Staggering* | Causing great astonishment or dismay; overwhelming |
| *Colossal* | Very great or impressive |
| *Reverses* | Changes to the opposite direction, position or condition |
| *Unswerving* | Firm and unchanging in intent or purpose |
| *Resolution* | Being resolved to do something; firm determination |
| *Subordinated* | Made secondary in importance |

## 53. So Much Hangs on the Fortunes of the Present Plan

In the year 1949, when construction began on the superstructure of the Shrine of the Báb, Shoghi Effendi wrote this to the National Spiritual Assembly of India:

> The sands are indeed running out. The task that remains to be accomplished is indeed colossal. The distractions, temptations, and pitfalls that might interfere with its consummation are many and varied. The resources however spiritual and material still at the disposal of the members of these communities, are still adequate, if they but resolve to utilize them, to the needs of the present hour. The blessings from on high, ready to be showered upon them, are more than adequate to ensure their complete and total victory. So much hangs on the fortunes of the present Plan! So much must necessarily depend on the manner and the spirit in which they discharge their terrific responsibilities, during the few fleeting months still allotted them ere the expiry of the Plan! I entreat them, with all the fervour of my soul, not to allow this golden opportunity to slip from their grasp. They have, in the past, proved themselves capable, in times of crisis, of overleaping the most formidable barriers, and of wresting victory from the jaws of impending defeat. Theirs is the opportunity, now if ever, to demonstrate a similar resolution, a no less spectacular outburst of enthusiasm, an even nobler heroism and self-sacrifice than they have ever shown in the past.
>
> Then, and only then, will the next stage in the evolution of their common destiny be unveiled to their eyes. Then, and only then, will the call summoning them to press forward to yet another landmark in their history be sounded. Then, and only then, will a still fuller measure of heavenly prizes be laid up for them in reward for their inestimable and arduous services in the treasuries of the Abhá Kingdom by Him who alone knows how to re-ignite His faithful servants.
>
> *(9 April 1949, DND 135-136)*

| | |
|---|---|
| *Colossal* | Unusually or impressively large |
| *Pitfalls* | Potential and usually unanticipated disasters or difficulties |
| *Consummation* | Completion; fulfillment of a goal |
| *Ensure* | To make sure that something will happen |
| *Fleeting* | Passing or fading quickly |

| | |
|---|---|
| *Allotted* | Distributed to somebody as a share of what is available or what has to be done |
| *Ere* | Before |
| *Expiry* | End, especially of a contract or agreement |
| *Wresting* | Taking something such as control or power from somebody in the face of opposition or resistance |
| *Impending* | About to happen |
| *Arduous* | Requiring hard work or continuous strenuous effort |

## 54. The Birth of the World Order

Just a few weeks after the second European Teaching Conference was held in Brussels, Shoghi Effendi wrote this to the Bahá'ís of Australia and New Zealand:

> Obstacles, varied and numerous, will no doubt arise to impede the onward march of this community. Reverses may temporarily dim the radiance of its mission. The forces of religious orthodoxy may well, at a future date, be leagued against it. The exponents of theories and doctrines fundamentally opposed to its religious tenets and social principles may challenge its infant strength with persistence and severity. The Administrative Order - the Ark destined to preserve its integrity and carry it to safety - must without delay, without exception, claim the attention of the members of this community, its ideals must be continually cherished in their hearts, its purposes studied and kept constantly before their eyes, its requirements wholeheartedly met, its laws scrupulously upheld, its institutions unstintingly supported, its glorious mission noised abroad, and its spirit made the sole motivating purpose of their lives.
>
> Then and only then, will this community, so young, so vibrant with life, so rich in promise, so dedicated to its task, be in a position to discharge adequately its weighty responsibilities, to reap the full harvest it has sown, acquire still greater potentialities for the conduct of subsequent stages in the crusade on which it has embarked, and contribute, to a degree unsuspected as yet by its members, its full share to the World-wide establishment of the Faith of Bahá'u'lláh, the emancipation of its Oriental followers, the recognition of its independence, the birth of its World Order and the emergence of that world civilization which that Order is destined to create.
>
> *(22 August 1949, LAN 80-81)*

| | |
|---|---|
| *Impede* | To interfere with the movement, progress or development of something |
| *Scrupulously* | Having moral integrity; acting in strict regard for what is considered right or proper |
| *Unstintingly* | Without restriction or holding back |
| *Noised Abroad* | Made generally known |

## 55. We Are Never to Hesitate

During 1952, Shoghi Effendi appointed the second contingent of Hands of the Cause of God and described their two-fold function: propagation of the Faith and preservation of its unity. He also described plans for the marble colonnade to encircle the Shrine of the Báb as an intermediate step to building a superstructure for the Shrine and sent his ideas to Italy for scale drawings and a price estimate; he announced the enlargement of the International Bahá'í Council to eight members; and he named the southern door of the Báb's tomb after Sutherland Maxwell, Hand of the Cause of God, who died in Montreal, in memory of his services. The case that had been brought against Shoghi Effendi by the Covenant-breakers in connection with the demolition of a house adjoining the Shrine and Mansion of Bahá'u'lláh at Bahjí was removed from the civil courts by the government of Israel. Midway in 1952, he wrote the Bahá'í world this message:

> No matter how long the period that separates them from ultimate victory; however arduous the task; however formidable the exertions demanded of them; however dark the days which mankind, perplexed and sorely-tried, must, in its hour of travail, traverse; however severe the tests with which they who are to redeem its fortunes will be confronted; however afflictive the darts which their present enemies, as well as those whom Providence, will, through His mysterious dispensations raise up from within or from without, may rain upon them, however grievous the ordeal of temporary separation from the heart and nerve-center of their Faith which future unforeseeable disturbances may impose upon them, I adjure them, by the precious blood that flowed in such great profusion, by the lives of the unnumbered saints and heroes who were immolated, by the supreme, the glorious sacrifice of the Prophet-Herald of our Faith, by the tribulations which its Founder, Himself, willingly underwent, so that His Cause might live, His Order might redeem a shattered world and its glory might suffuse the entire planet - I adjure them, as this solemn hour draws nigh, to resolve never to flinch, never to hesitate, never to relax, until each and every objective in the Plans to be proclaimed, at a later date, has been fully consummated.
>
> *(30 June 1952 MBW 38-39)*

| | |
|---|---|
| *Arduous* | Requiring hard work or continuous strenuous effort |
| *Formidable* | Difficult to deal with or overcome |
| *Exertions* | Strenuous physical exercise or effort |

| | |
|---|---|
| *Sorely-tried* | Made to undergo extreme trials or distress |
| *Travail* | Painful effort; anguish |
| *Traverse* | Pass through |
| *Severe* | Difficult to do or endure |
| *Redeem* | To help to overcome something which causes harm |
| *Afflictive* | Causing severe mental or physical distress to somebody |
| *Providence* | God, conceived as the power sustaining and guiding human destiny |
| *Dispensations* | Particular arrangements or provisions, especially of providence or nature |
| *Grievous* | Very severe or serious |
| *Ordeal* | A severe trial or experience |
| *Impose* | To establish or bring about as if by force |
| *Adjure* | To make an earnest appeal to somebody |
| *Profusion* | A large quantity of something |
| *Immolated* | Offered in sacrifice; killed |
| *Supreme* | Greatest in importance and significance; ultimate |
| *Shattered* | Broken into pieces; seriously damaged |
| *Suffuse* | To spread through or over something completely |
| *Solemn* | Deeply serious |
| *Resolve* | Make a decision |
| *Flinch* | To avoid thinking about something, confronting something, or doing something |
| *Consummated* | Completed or fulfilled, especially something long desired |

## 56. The Tribulations Suffered by Their Co-Religionists

**In the** same month that Shoghi Effendi wrote the following letter to the British Isles, appeals were made by National Spiritual Assemblies around the world through the Bahá'í International Community to the UN Secretary General Dag Hammarskjold to ask the Iranian government to halt the attacks on the Bahá'ís. This marks the first time that the Faith was able to defend itself with its newly-born administrative agencies. An "Aid the Persecuted Fund" was established:

> The efforts of the members of this community must indeed be redoubled, nay trebled, as they view with afflicted hearts the tragic trend of events transpiring with such dramatic and sudden swiftness in Bahá'u'lláh's native land. The tribulations suffered, over so wide a field, by so many of their co-religionists, under circumstances so appalling and harrowing in their nature, at the hands of redoubtable, pitiless, barbarous adversaries, should spur them on to still greater endeavours in a land blessed with freedom of religion and tolerance, and occupying so conspicuous a position among its sister nations.
>
> Theirs is an opportunity which they must instantly grasp. Theirs is a responsibility which they cannot escape. Theirs is the duty to offset, by the quality of their achievements, the dire losses which are now being sustained in the cradle of the Faith. That they may in every field and at all times discharge their heavy responsibilities is my constant prayer and dearest hope.
>
> *(5 August 1955 UD 355)*

| | |
|---|---|
| *Afflicted* | Severely distressed, enough to cause persistent suffering or anguish |
| *Transpiring* | Happening |
| *Appalling* | Dreadful and shocking |
| *Harrowing* | Causing feelings of fear, horror or distress |
| *Redoubtable* | Formidable; arousing fear or awe |
| *Spur on* | To incite or stimulate to action, e.g. because of the hope of a reward or the fear of punishment |
| *Conspicuous* | Attracting attention through being unusual or remarkable |
| *Offset* | To counterbalance or compensate for something |
| *Dire* | Characterized by severe, serious or desperate circumstances |

## 57. Our Faith Must Be Indomitable

**After** Shoghi Effendi announced in April of 1957 that the Faith had been established in 251 countries, that there were more than a thousand local spiritual assemblies, that Bahá'ís lived in more than 4,200 localities and that every territory mentioned in the Tablets of the Divine Plan had been opened to the Faith and Bahá'í literature had been translated into 230 languages, he wrote in June to the National Assembly of Alaska:

> The task now facing this highly promising, spiritually dynamic community, at the hour of its emergence as an independent member of the embryonic World Bahá'í Commonwealth, is truly formidable; the responsibilities which it valiantly shoulders, at this crucial hour in its evolution are sacred, heavy, manifold and inescapable. The tests and trials which it must, sooner or later, experience in the course of its unfoldment and consolidation will severely challenge its spirit and resources. The path which it must tread ere the full evidence of its latent capacities are manifested will be long, tortuous and stony. The indomitable faith which now so powerfully animates its members, however, will, beyond the shadow of a doubt, enable them to overcome whatever obstacles may confront them in the future, and ensure the ultimate attainment of their high destiny.
>
> *(30 June 1957, HE 37)*

| | |
|---|---|
| *Emergence* | The act or process of coming out, appearing or coming about |
| *Embryonic* | In an initial or rudimentary stage of development |
| *Commonwealth* | An association of countries that have joined together for their common good |
| *Formidable* | Difficult to deal with or overcome |
| *Valiantly* | Courageously |
| *Shoulders* | Takes on the responsibility for something, especially something unpleasant or worrying |
| *Inescapable* | Impossible to avoid |
| *Ere* | Before |
| *Latent* | Present or existing, but in an underdeveloped or unexpressed form |
| *Tortuous* | Marked by repeated twists, bends or turns |
| *Indomitable* | Brave, determined and impossible to defeat or frighten |
| *Animates* | Inspires to take action or to have strong feelings |

| | |
|---|---|
| *Confront* | To be met face to face by something that must be overcome |
| *Ensure* | To make sure that something will happen |
| *Ultimate* | Coming or expected at the very end |
| *Attainment* | The achievement of the goals that somebody has set |
| *Destiny* | The inner purpose of a life that can be discovered and realized |

Photograph by Nayyirih G. de Koning-Tahzib

# The Course of Change

> You must be the change you want to see in the world
> *Mahatma Gandhi*

> There are three constants in life… change, choice and principles.
> *Stephen R. Covey, American Speaker /Trainer*
> *Author of "The 7 Habits of Highly Effective People"*

LIFE is constantly changing, and the needs and times of the various Plans of the Faith change and evolve. We need to follow in the mainstream of the Faith and be aware of what is being asked of us at a particular time. By doing this we will be protected from negativism and remain full of hope and conviction that even though the course of worldly events seems hopeless, God's ultimate Plan for humankind will be achieved if we arise and do all we can to help bring this about.

## 58. Looking Towards the Future

**Shoghi** Effendi returned in September 1924 to the Holy Land after an absence of some six months when he wrote this to the Bahá'ís throughout the Continent of America:

> And now as I look into the future, I hope to see the friends at all times, in every land, and of every shade of thought and character, voluntarily and joyously rallying round their local and in particular their national centers of activity, upholding and promoting their interests with complete unanimity and contentment, with perfect understanding, genuine enthusiasm, and sustained vigor. This indeed is the one joy and yearning of my life, for it is the fountainhead from which all future blessings will flow, the broad foundation upon which the security of the Divine Edifice must ultimately rest. May we not hope that now at last the dawn of a brighter day is breaking upon our beloved Cause?
>
> *(24 September 1924, BA 67)*

| | |
|---|---|
| *Rallying* | Coming together in order to provide support or make a shared effort |
| *Fountainhead* | The primary source |
| *Edifice* | An elaborate, complicated structure of ideas |

## 59. If We Fail To Play Our Part

**AFTER** Shoghi Effendi returned to the Holy Land after an absence of some six months, he wrote to the Bahá'ís of America:

> Humanity, through suffering and turmoil, is swiftly moving on towards its destiny; if we be loiterers, if we fail to play our part surely others will be called upon to take up our task as ministers to the crying needs of this afflicted world.
>
> Not by the force of numbers, not by the mere exposition of a set of new and noble principles, not by an organized campaign of teaching - no matter how worldwide and elaborate in its character - not even by the staunchness of our faith or the exaltation of our enthusiasm, can we ultimately hope to vindicate in the eyes of a critical and sceptical age the supreme claim of the Abha Revelation. One thing and only one thing will unfailingly and alone secure the undoubted triumph of this sacred Cause, namely, the extent to which our own inner life and private character mirror forth in their manifold aspects the splendor of those eternal principles proclaimed by Bahá'u'lláh.
>
> *(24 September 924, BA 66)*

| | |
|---|---|
| *Turmoil* | A state of great confusion, commotion or disturbance |
| *Swiftly* | Very quickly |
| *Destiny* | A predetermined and inevitable series of events beyond human control |
| *Loiterers* | People who do something in a slow lazy way, often stopping to rest |
| *Afflicted* | Experiencing severe mental or physical distress |
| *Mere* | Just what is specified and nothing more |
| *Exposition* | Detailed description or discussion |
| *Elaborate* | Planned or organized with thoroughness and careful attention to detail |
| *Staunchness* | Showing loyalty, dependability and enthusiasm |
| *Exaltation* | A feeling of intense or excessive happiness or exhilaration |
| *Enthusiasm* | Passionate interest in or eagerness to do something |
| *Ultimately* | In the end, as the culmination of a process or event |
| *Vindicate* | To justify or prove the worth of something |
| *Sceptical* | Showing doubt |

| | |
|---|---|
| *Supreme* | Greater than any that have gone before, or the greatest possible |
| *Claim* | A statement of something as a fact, saying it is true |
| *Secure* | To bring about; make something happen |
| *Extent* | The degree to which something applies |
| *Mirror forth* | Reflect like in a mirror; show as an example |
| *Manifold* | Having many parts, forms or applications |
| *Aspects* | Particular views or points of view |
| *Splendor* | Magnificence, impressiveness or brilliance |

## 60. The Significance of Our Undertaking

**The** intended pilgrimage of Queen Marie of Romania to the Bahá'í Shrines was thwarted during March 1938 when Shoghi Effendi wrote to the Bahá'ís of the West:

> Feeble though our Faith may now appear in the eyes of men, who either denounce it as an offshoot of Islam, or contemptuously ignore it as one more of those obscure sects that abound in the West, this priceless gem of Divine Revelation, now still in its embryonic state, shall evolve within the shell of His law, and shall forge ahead, undivided and unimpaired, till it embraces the whole of mankind. Only those who have already recognized the supreme station of Bahá'u'lláh, only those whose hearts have been touched by His love, and have become familiar with the potency of His spirit, can adequately appreciate the value of this Divine Economy - His inestimable gift to mankind.
>
> Leaders of religion, exponents of political theories, governors of human institutions, who at present are witnessing with perplexity and dismay the bankruptcy of their ideas, and the disintegration of their handiwork, would do well to turn their gaze to the Revelation of Bahá'u'lláh, and to meditate upon the World Order which, lying enshrined in His teachings, is slowly and imperceptibly rising amid the welter and chaos of present-day civilization. They need have no doubt or anxiety regarding the nature, the origin or validity of the institutions which the adherents of the Faith are building up throughout the world. For these lie embedded in the teachings themselves, unadulterated and unobscured by unwarrantable inferences, or unauthorized interpretations of His Word.
>
> *(21 March 1930, WOB 23-24)*

| | |
|---|---|
| *Denounce* | To criticize something publicly |
| *Offshoot* | Something that has grown out of something else |
| *Contemptuously* | Demonstrating a strong dislike or utter lack of respect |
| *Obscure* | Unimportant or unknown |
| *Abound* | To be present in large numbers or quantities |
| *Unimpaired* | Not badly affected by anything unpleasant or dangerous that happens |
| *Perplexity* | A state of feeling confused or puzzled |
| *Imperceptibly* | So slightly or gradually that it is hard to notice |
| *Welter* | Confused condition |
| *Unadulterated* | Pure |
| *Unobscured* | Clear; not hidden |

| | |
|---|---|
| *Unwarrantable* | Unable to be justified; inexcusable |
| *Inferences* | Conclusions drawn from evidence or reasoning |

## 61. The Goal of a New World Order

**When** Shoghi Effendi wrote these World Order letters to fellow believers in the Faith in November of 1931, the New York Bahá'í community drafted the by-laws of a Bahá'í local assembly. These became the pattern for all local Bahá'í constitutions throughout the world.

> Humanity, whether viewed in the light of man's individual conduct or in the existing relationships between organized communities and nations, has, alas, strayed too far and suffered too great a decline to be redeemed through the unaided efforts of the best among its recognized rulers and statesmen - however disinterested their motives, however concerted their action, however unsparing in their zeal and devotion to its cause. No scheme which the calculations of the highest statesmanship may yet devise; no doctrine which the most distinguished exponents of economic theory may hope to advance; no principle which the most ardent of moralists may strive to inculcate, can provide, in the last resort, adequate foundations upon which the future of a distracted world can be built. No appeal for mutual tolerance which the worldly-wise might raise, however compelling and insistent, can calm its passions or help restore its vigor. Nor would any general scheme of mere organized international cooperation, in whatever sphere of human activity, however ingenious in conception, or extensive in scope, succeed in removing the root cause of the evil that has so rudely upset the equilibrium of present-day society. Not even, I venture to assert, would the very act of devising the machinery required for the political and economic unification of the world - a principle that has been increasingly advocated in recent times - provide in itself the antidote against the poison that is steadily undermining the vigor of organized peoples and nations. What else, might we not confidently affirm, but the unreserved acceptance of the Divine Program enunciated, with such simplicity and force as far back as sixty years ago, by Bahá'u'lláh, embodying in its essentials God's divinely appointed scheme for the unification of mankind in this age, coupled with an indomitable conviction in the unfailing efficacy of each and all of its provisions, is eventually capable of withstanding the forces of internal disintegration which, if unchecked, must needs continue to eat into the vitals of a despairing society. It is towards this goal - the goal of a new World Order, Divine in origin, all-embracing in scope, equitable in principle, challenging in its features - that a harassed humanity must strive.
>
> *(29 November 1931, WOB 33-34)*

| | |
|---|---|
| *Strayed* | Wandered away from the right path |
| *Unsparing* | Giving generously or liberally |
| *Devise* | Invent, make up or put together |
| *Exponents* | Supporters or promoters of an idea |
| *Ardent* | Feeling or showing great enthusiasm or eagerness |
| *Inculcate* | To fix something firmly in somebody's mind through frequent, forceful repetition |
| *Ingenious* | Clever, original and effective |
| *Venture* | To be so bold as to; to dare |
| *Antidote* | A substance that counteracts poison |
| *Embodying* | Making things into an organized system or whole |
| *Indomitable* | Brave, determined and impossible to defeat or frighten |
| *Efficacy* | The power of producing an effect; effectiveness |
| *Vitals* | The parts necessary for functioning, as of a system |
| *Equitable* | Fair |
| *Harassed* | Anxious, annoyed and tired |

## 62. The Bedrock on Which This Administrative Order Is Founded

In this year of 1934, a month before Shoghi Effendi wrote this to the Bahá'ís of the West, he gave Queen Marie of Romania the gift of a Tablet in the handwriting of Bahá'u'lláh:

> Let no one, while this System is still in its infancy, misconceive its character, belittle its significance or misrepresent its purpose. The bedrock on which this Administrative Order is founded is God's immutable Purpose for mankind in this day. The Source from which it derives its inspiration is no one less than Bahá'u'lláh Himself. Its shield and defender are the embattled hosts of the Abhá Kingdom. Its seed is the blood of no less than twenty thousand martyrs who have offered up their lives that it may be born and flourish. The axis round which its institutions revolve are the authentic provisions of the Will and Testament of 'Abdu'l-Bahá. Its guiding principles are the truths which He Who is the unerring Interpreter of the teachings of our Faith has so clearly enunciated in His public addresses throughout the West. The laws that govern its operation and limit its functions are those which have been expressly ordained in the Kitáb-i-Aqdas. The seat round which its spiritual, its humanitarian and administrative activities will cluster are the Mashriqu'l-Adhkár and its Dependencies. The pillars that sustain its authority and buttress its structure are the twin institutions of the Guardianship and of the Universal House of Justice. The central, the underlying aim which animates it is the establishment of the New World Order as adumbrated by Bahá'u'lláh. The methods it employs, the standard it inculcates, incline it to neither East nor West, neither Jew nor Gentile, neither rich nor poor, neither white nor colored. Its watchword is the unification of the human race; its standard the "Most Great Peace"; its consummation the advent of that golden millennium - the Day when the kingdoms of this world shall have become the Kingdom of God Himself, the Kingdom of Bahá'u'lláh.
>
> *(8 February 1934, WOB 156-157)*

| | |
|---|---|
| *Misconceive* | Fail to understand |
| *Belittle* | Reduce or dismiss the importanc or quality of something |
| *Bedrock* | The foundation; underlying facts and principles |
| *Immutable* | Unchanging or unchangeable |
| *Derives* | Gets; receives |
| *Embattled* | Under attack |
| *Hosts* | A very large number of people |

| | |
|---|---|
| *Flourish* | Be healthy or grow well |
| *Axis* | The line around which objects rotate |
| *Provisions* | Things that have been given |
| *Unerring* | Accurate; making no mistakes |
| *Enunciated* | Stated precisely and systematically |
| *Ordained* | Formally commanded |
| *Buttress* | Give support to |
| *Animates* | Gives life to; inspires to action |
| *Adumbrated* | Disclosed partially or guardedly; shown in outline |
| *Inculcates* | Fixes firmly in one's mind |

## 63. Evidences of a Splendid Power

**Shoghi** Effendi wrote this letter to the Bahá'ís of the West in the year 1934, when the world situation was worsening and the government in Iran took several measures against the Bahá'ís throughout the country: nineteen Bahá'í schools were closed; Bahá'í meetings were forbidden in many towns; 3 Bahá'í centres were closed; some Bahá'í military were stripped of their rank and imprisoned; Bahá'ís in many places were harassed over the filling-in of marriage certificates, census forms and other legal documents, and despite all this the first National Spiritual Assembly of Iran was elected.

> The vitality which the organic institutions of this great, this ever-expanding Order so strongly exhibit; the obstacles which the high courage, the undaunted resolution of its administrators have already surmounted; the fire of an unquenchable enthusiasm that glows with undiminished fervor in the hearts of its itinerant teachers; the heights of self-sacrifice which its champion-builders are now attaining; the breadth of vision, the confident hope, the creative joy, the inward peace, the uncompromising integrity, the exemplary discipline, the unyielding unity and solidarity which its stalwart defenders manifest; the degree to which its moving Spirit has shown itself capable of assimilating the diversified elements within its pale, of cleansing them of all forms of prejudice and of fusing them with its own structure - these are evidences of a power which a disillusioned and sadly shaken society can ill afford to ignore.

> Compare these splendid manifestations of the spirit animating this vibrant body of the Faith of Bahá'u'lláh with the cries and agony, the follies and vanities, the bitterness and prejudices, the wickedness and divisions of an ailing and chaotic world. Witness the fear that torments its leaders and paralyzes the action of its blind and bewildered statesmen. How fierce the hatreds, how false the ambitions, how petty the pursuits, how deep-rooted the suspicions of its peoples! How disquieting the lawlessness, the corruption, the unbelief that are eating into the vitals of a tottering civilization!

> Might not this process of steady deterioration which is insidiously invading so many departments of human activity and thought be regarded as a necessary accompaniment to the rise of this almighty Arm of Bahá'u'lláh? Might we not look upon the momentous happenings which, in the course of the past twenty years, have so deeply agitated every continent of the earth, as ominous signs simultaneously proclaiming the agonies of a disintegrating civilization and the birth

pangs of that World Order - that Ark of human salvation - that must needs arise upon its ruins?

*(8 February 1934, WOB 155)*

| | |
|---|---|
| *Ever-expanding* | Increasing continuously in size and *scope* |
| | *Undaunted*   Not afraid or deterred by the prospect of defeat, loss or failure |
| *Resolution* | Firm determination to do something |
| *Surmounted* | Dealt with successfully, as with a difficulty |
| *Unquenchable* | Impossible to suppress or destroy |
| *Undiminished* | Not reduced or lessened |
| *Fervor* | Intense emotion; passion *Itinerant* Traveling from place to place |
| *Uncompromising* | Having beliefs that are fixed and do not change, especially when faced with opposition |
| *Integrity* | The quality of possessing and steadfastly adhering to high moral principles |
| *Unyielding* | Not giving in to persuasion, pressure or force |
| *Stalwart defenders* | Faithful, dependable and hard-working supporters |
| *Pale* | A region within enclosed boundaries |
| *Petty* | Of little importance |
| *Insidiously* | Slowly and subtly harmful or destructive |
| *Ominous* | Menacing; threatening |

## 64. A New Stage in Concentrated Teaching Activity

**Shortly** before Martha Root met with Queen Marie of Romania in 1936 for the eighth and last time, Shoghi Effendi penned these words to the American Bahá'ís:

> This new stage in the gradual unfoldment of the Formative Period of our Faith into which we have just entered - the phase of concentrated teaching activity - synchronizes with a period of deepening gloom, of universal impotence, of ever-increasing destitution and widespread disillusionment in the fortunes of a declining age. This is truly providential and its significance and the opportunities it offers us should be fully apprehended and utilized. Now that the administrative organs of a firmly established Faith are vigorously and harmoniously functioning, and now that the Symbol (i.e., the House of Worship) of its invincible might is lending unprecedented impetus to its spread, an effort unexampled in its scope and sustained vitality is urgently required so that the moving spirit of its Founder may permeate and transform the lives of the countless multitudes that hunger for its teachings. That the beloved friends in America, who have carried triumphantly the banner of His Cause through the initial stages of its development, will in a still greater measure prove themselves capable of meeting the challenge of the present hour, I, for one, can never doubt. Of the evidences of their inexhaustible vitality I am sufficiently and continually conscious. My fervent plea will not, I feel certain, remain unanswered. For them I shall continue to pray from all my heart.
>
> *(10 January 1936, MA 18)*

| | |
|---|---|
| *Gloom* | A feeling or atmosphere of despair, despondency or misery |
| *Impotence* | Powerlessness |
| *Destitution* | Extreme poverty |
| *Declining* | Decreasing in number, amount, value or quality |
| *Providential* | Happening exactly when needed but without being planned |
| *Apprehended* | To grasp the importance, significance or meaning of something |
| *Utilized* | Make use of |
| *Vigorously* | Displaying or using great energy |
| *Invincible* | Unbeatable |
| *Lending* | Giving a particular quality of character to something |
| *Unprecedented* | Having no earlier parallel or equivalent |

| | | | |
|---|---|---|---|
| *Impetus* | A driving force | *Scope* | Breadth, or opportunity to function |
| *Permeate* | Spread throughout | | |

## 65. The Leaven that Must Leaven the Lump

**Written** a few months after the passing of Muníríh Khánum, the Holy Mother, on 30 April 1938 and several weeks before Queen Marie of Romania passed away on 25 July 1938, Shoghi Effendi wrote this to the Bahá'ís of North America:

> Pregnant indeed are the years looming ahead of us all. The twin processes of internal disintegration and external chaos are being accelerated and every day are inexorably moving towards a climax. The rumblings that must precede the eruption of those forces that must cause "the limbs of humanity to quake" can already be heard. "The time of the end," "the latter years," as foretold in the Scriptures, are at long last upon us. The Pen of Bahá'u'lláh, the voice of 'Abdu'l-Bahá, have time and again, insistently and in terms unmistakable, warned an unheeding humanity of impending disaster. The Community of the Most Great Name, the leaven that must leaven the lump, the chosen remnant that must survive the rolling up of the old, discredited, tottering order, and assist in the unfoldment of a new one in its stead, is standing ready, alert, clear-visioned, and resolute. The American believers, standard-bearers of this world-wide community and torch-bearers of an as yet unborn civilization, have girt up their loins, unfurled their banners and stepped into the arena of service. Their Plan has been formulated. Their forces are mobilized. They are steadfastly marching towards their goal. The hosts of the Abhá Kingdom are rushing forth, as promised, to direct their steps and reinforce their power. Through their initial victories they have provided the impulse that must now surge and, with relentless force sweep over their sister-communities and eventually overpower the entire human race. The generality of mankind, blind and enslaved, is wholly unaware of the healing power with which this community has been endowed, nor can it as yet suspect the role which this same community is destined to play in its redemption.
>
> Fierce and manifold will be the assaults with which governments, races, classes and religions, jealous of its rising prestige and fearful of its consolidating strength, will seek to silence its voice and sap its foundations. Unmoved by the relative obscurity that surrounds it at the present time, and undaunted by the forces that will be arrayed against it in the future, this community, I cannot but feel confident, will, no matter how afflictive the agonies of a travailing age, pursue its destiny, undeflected in its course, undimmed in its serenity, unyielding in its resolve, unshaken in its convictions.
>
> *(5 July 1938, MA 33)*

| | |
|---|---|
| *Looming* | Something about to happen that seems threatening |
| *Inexorably* | Impossible to stop |
| *Rumblings* | First indications |
| *Unheeding* | Not paying attention *Impending* Threatening to happen |
| *Leaven* | 1. Something that lightens things, like yeast. 2. To modify or lighten |
| *Remnant* | A small part of something that remains after the rest has gone |
| *Tottering* | Unstable or on the point of collapse |
| *Stead* | In place of another |
| *Resolute* | Characterized by determination |
| *Standard-bearers* | Leaders |
| *Torch-bearers* | Sources of enlightenment |
| *Girt up their loins* | Prepared and strengthened themselves to do something difficult and challenging |
| *Unfurled* | Spread out Rushing *forth* Moving forward quickly |
| *Surge* | Increase suddenly |
| *Relentless* | Ceaseless and intense |
| *Sweep* | Move with speed and force |
| *Endowed* | Having been given a particular quality or feature |
| *Suspect* | Believe to be probable or possible |
| *Redemption* | A thing that saves someone from error or evil |
| *Fierce* | Violent or intense |
| *Assaults* | Violent physical or verbal attacks |
| *Sap* | Drain of strength or power |
| *Undaunted* | Not afraid or deterred by the prospect of defeat, loss or failure |
| *Arrayed* | To set out a large number or wide range of people |
| *Travailing* | Working hard or with pain |
| *Undeflected* | Not turning aside, especially from a straight course or fixed direction |

## 66. Undreamt of Opportunities Offered

In 1938 Baháʼís in the Soviet Union were persecuted by the authorities; five hundred Baháʼí men were imprisoned in Turkistan; many Iranian Baháʼís living in various cities of the Soviet Union were arrested; some were sent to Siberia, others to Pavladar in northern Kazakhstan and others to Iran; six hundred refugee Baháʼís – women, girls, children and a few old men – went to Iran, mostly to Mashhad; the Baháʼí Temple in ʻIshqábád was confiscated and turned into an art gallery; the Baháʼí schools were ordered closed and Spiritual Assemblies and all administrative institutions in the Caucasus were dissolved. At this time Shoghi Effendi wrote the following to the United States and Canada:

> The field is indeed so immense, the period so critical, the Cause so great, the workers so few, the time so short, the privilege so priceless, that no follower of the Faith of Baháʼu'lláh, worthy to bear His name, can afford a moment's hesitation. That God-born Force, irresistible in its sweeping power, incalculable in its potency, unpredictable in its course, mysterious in its workings, and awe-inspiring in its manifestations - a Force which, as the Báb has written, "vibrates within the innermost being of all created things," and which, according to Baháʼu'lláh, has through its "vibrating influence," "upset the equilibrium of the world and revolutionized its ordered life" - such a Force, acting even as a two-edged sword, is, under our very eyes, sundering, on the one hand, the age-old ties which for centuries have held together the fabric of civilized society, and is unloosing, on the other, the bonds that still fetter the infant and as yet unemancipated Faith of Baháʼu'lláh. The undreamt-of opportunities offered through the operation of this Force - the American believers must now rise, and fully and courageously exploit them. "The holy realities of the Concourse on high," writes ʻAbduʼl-Bahá, "yearn, in this day, in the Most Exalted Paradise, to return unto this world, so that they may be aided to render some service to the threshold of the Abha Beauty, and arise to demonstrate their servitude to His sacred Threshold."
>
> (25 December 1938, ADJ 39)

| | |
|---|---|
| *Sweeping* | On a large scale |
| *Sundering* | Separating something into parts, especially by force |
| *Fetter* | Restrict the freedom of; restrain and confine |
| *Exploit* | Use something for benefit |

## 67. The One Refuge

**In 1941** John Henry Hyde Dunn, Hand of the Cause of God, died in Sydney in February. In May of the same year, Yvonne Cuellar, a Frenchwoman, became the first Bahá'í to pioneer to Bolivia; Shoghi Effendi called her the 'Mother of Bolivia'. And it was in March of that year that Shoghi Effendi wrote this to the Bahá'ís of the West:

> We are indeed living in an age which, if we would correctly appraise it, should be regarded as one which is witnessing a dual phenomenon. The first signalizes the death pangs of an order, effete and godless, that has stubbornly refused, despite the signs and portents of a century-old Revelation, to attune its processes to the precepts and ideals which that Heaven-sent Faith proffered it. The second proclaims the birth pangs of an Order, divine and redemptive, that will inevitably supplant the former, and within Whose administrative structure an embryonic civilization, incomparable and world-embracing, is imperceptibly maturing. The one is being rolled up, and is crashing in oppression, bloodshed, and ruin. The other opens up vistas of a justice, a unity, a peace, a culture, such as no age has ever seen. The former has spent its force, demonstrated its falsity and barrenness, lost irretrievably its opportunity, and is hurrying to its doom. The latter, virile and unconquerable, is plucking asunder its chains, and is vindicating its title to be the one refuge within which a sore-tried humanity, purged from its dross, can attain its destiny.
>
> *(28 March 1941, PDC 16)*

| | |
|---|---|
| *Appraise* | To form or give an opinion of something's quality |
| *Effete* | Characterized by decadence, triviality or self-indulgence |
| *Portents* | Indications that something, often something unpleasant, is going to happen |
| *Precepts* | Rules, instructions or principles that guide someone's actions, especially those that guide moral behavior |
| *Proffered* | Held something out so it could be accepted |
| *Supplant* | Replace |
| *Imperceptibly* | Very slightly or gradually |
| *Irretrievably* | Impossible to get back or recover |
| *Virile* | Showing energy, power and forcefulness |
| *Plucking* | Taking something away quickly |
| *Asunder* | Into different parts or pieces |

| | |
|---|---|
| *Vindicating* | Defending or maintaining the recognition of something, such as a cause or one's rights |
| *Purged* | Purified; freed from undesirable aspects |
| *Dross* | Worthless matter |

## 68. We are Destined to Achieve Memorable Victories

In 1946, the restoration of the House of Bahá'u'lláh in Tihrán was completed; Shoghi Effendi instructed Sutherland Maxwell to set plans in motion for the first stages of the building of the superstructure of the Shrine of the Báb; and the Second Seven Year Plan of the United States and Canada was launched. In April, the National Spiritual Assembly of Germany and Austria was established, and one month later, Shoghi Effendi appended this letter to the new National Assembly:

> My heart rejoiced and my soul was refreshed at the receipt of your most welcome message, signed by so great a number of ardent and youthful co-workers in a land so rich in promise, so blessed by our Beloved, and so severely tried by the vicissitudes of war. You are, I assure you, often in my thoughts and prayers, and I cherish the brightest hopes for your future work. You are, I feel confident, destined to achieve memorable victories, both in your native land and on the continent of Europe, and you should diligently and unitedly prepare yourselves for this glorious task. Persevere, redouble your efforts, and rest assured that the Beloved will bless and sustain you always.
>
> *(4 May 1946, LDG Vol. I 106)*

| | |
|---|---|
| *Ardent* | Feeling or showing great enthusiasm or eagerness |
| *Vicissitudes* | Unexpected changes, especially in somebody's fortunes |
| *Diligently* | Showing persistent and hard-working effort in doing something |
| *Sustain* | Support and encourange; keep in existence |

## 69. Great Work To Be Undertaken in the Future

**During** the same year, 1946, that the National Spiritual Assembly of Germany and Austria was established, the restoration of the House of Bahá'u'lláh in Tihrán was completed, and Shoghi Effendi wrote to the National Spiritual Assembly of the British Isles:

> The evidences of intensified activity and of notable progress on the part of the English believers in recent months have rejoiced my heart and deepened my feelings of admiration and gratitude for the manner in which they are discharging, individually and collectively, their high responsibilities. I long to hear of the steady progress of their Plan, and will continue to pray for the removal of every obstacle in their path. However considerable their recent achievements, they are still in the initial stage of their great unfolding mission, and are not even capable as yet of visualising the possibilities or of estimating the consequences of their present-day labours. The consummation of their present task will mark the opening of a new era in the development of their community and will signalise the inauguration of a great epoch in the history of the Faith in their land--an epoch that must witness the universal recognition of their Cause and the proclamation of its truths, its claims and tenets, to the masses of their countrymen throughout the British Isles. The Plan they are now prosecuting will provide the machinery and establish the basic structure that will enable them to arouse the people, among all sections of the population, and aid them, systematically and gradually, to recognise Bahá'u'lláh, and support the nascent institutions of this World Order. Now it is their duty to lay an unassailable foundation for the great work that is to be undertaken in the future. There is no time to lose. Theirs is a priceless opportunity and a great privilege. They must neither vacillate nor falter. They must determinedly persevere until their immediate and distant goals have been attained.
>
> *(12 October 1946, UD 191-192)*

| | |
|---|---|
| *Notable* | Significant or great enough to deserve attention or to be recorded |
| *Discharging* | Carrying out a duty, responsibility or promise |
| *Signalise* | Make remarkable or conspicuous |
| *Inauguration* | The beginning of a new period, style or activity |
| *Epoch* | A period of history, especially one in which there are new advances and great change |
| *Tenets* | Doctrines or principles |
| *Prosecuting* | Carrying out until completion; following to the end |

| | |
|---|---|
| *Nascent* | Just beginning to develop; emerging |
| *Unassailable* | So sound or well established that it cannot be challenged or denied |
| *Vacillate* | To swing indecisively in choice of opinions or actions |
| *Falter* | To be unsteady in purpose or action; stumble |
| *Persevere* | To persist steadily in an action or belief, usually over a long period and especially despite roblems or difficulties |

## 70. The Champion-Builders of Bahá'u'lláh's Embryonic Order

In the spring of 1947, the National Spiritual Assembly of the United States and Canada was accredited by the United Nations as a non-governmental organization. Shoghi Effendi wrote this to the Bahá'ís of the West:

> Invested, among its sister communities in East and West, with the primacy conferred upon it by 'Abdu'l-Bahá's Divine Plan; armed with the mandatory provisions of His momentous Tablets; equipped with the agencies of a quarter-century-old Administrative Order, whose fabric it has reared and consolidated; encouraged by the marvelous success achieved by its daughter communities throughout the Americas, a success which has sealed the triumph of the first stage of that Plan; launched on a campaign of vaster dimensions, of superior merit, of weightier potentialities, than any it has hitherto initiated, a campaign destined to multiply its spiritual progeny in distant lands and amidst divers races, the community of the Most Great Name in the North American continent must arise, as it has never before in its history, and demonstrate anew its capacity to perform such deeds as are worthy of its high calling. Its members, the executors of 'Abdu'l-Bahá's Plan, the champion-builders of Bahá'u'lláh's embryonic Order, the torchbearers of a world-girdling civilization, must, in the years immediately ahead, bestir themselves, and, as bidden by 'Abdu'l-Bahá, "increase" their exertions "a thousandfold," lay bare further vistas in the "range" of their "future achievements" and of their "unspeakably glorious" mission, and hasten the day when, as prophesied by Him, their community will "find itself securely established upon the throne of an everlasting dominion," when "the whole earth" will be stirred and shaken by the results of its "achievements" and "resound with the praises of majesty and greatness," when America will "evolve into a center from which waves of spiritual power will emanate, and the throne of the Kingdom of God will, in the plenitude of its majesty and glory, be firmly established."
>
> *(5 June 1947, CF 30-31)*

| | |
|---|---|
| *Invested* | Provided with a particular quality or characteristic |
| *Primacy* | Being first or foremost |
| *Conferred* | Given an honor or title |
| *Mandatory* | Needing to be done, followed or complied with, usually because of an official requirement |

| | |
|---|---|
| *Momentous* | Extremely important or crucial, especially in the effect on the future course of events |
| *Fabric* | The fundamental structure or makeup of something |
| *Hitherto* | Up to the present time or the time in question |
| *Progeny* | Offspring or descendants |
| *Girdling* | Something that surrounds or encircles something else |
| *Bestir* | Become active; start doing something |
| *Vistas* | Mental pictures covering a long succession of events in the past or the future |

## 71. Torch-Bearers of the Light of Divine Guidance

In September 1947, George Townshend, at the age of 71 years, resigned his position with the Church of Ireland. He was the first ordained priest of a Christian Protestant church to renounce his Orders and to become a fully accredited member of the Bahá'í community. A month later, Shoghi Effendi appended this to the National Spiritual Assembly of Germany and Austria:

> The spirit which the entire body of the German believers have displayed, despite the hardships and trials which they have heroically endured, and are still enduring, is a magnificent example to their fellow-workers in both the East and the West, a source of great inspiration to me, and a magnet that will powerfully attract the blessings of the Almighty. My thoughts, though I myself am immersed in an ocean of work and preoccupations, often turn in loving admiration and gratitude to those who, for more than a decade, have in the face of constant peril, held fast to the Faith of God, who have survived the greatest ordeal that has ever afflicted the Faith of Bahá'u'lláh in the West, and who are now forging ahead, united, resolved and consecrated, in the path leading to still greater victories.
>
> ... The path you are treading is hard and stony and beset with many pitfalls. The tasks you are called upon to discharge are varied, complex, urgent and gigantic. The resources at your disposal are meagre. The hour, however, for raising the call of Bahá'u'lláh is propitious. The hearts of your countrymen, prepared by bewilderment and suffering, are ready to respond to His message. You stand at the threshold of a new and glorious era in the evolution of His Faith in that land. The opportunities of the present hour are priceless and may never recur again. Time is pressing. The eyes of your fellow-workers in both Hemispheres are fixed upon you. Our beloved Master who showered, through His visit and His messages to you, so much love and encouragement and so many blessings, is watching over you from on high, ready to sustain your efforts and lead you on to victory.
>
> That you may rise to still greater heights of heroism, that you may discharge befittingly your sacred responsibilities, that you may adorn the annals of your Faith with still greater evidences of your devotion, courage and perseverance, that you may achieve your high destiny as the torch-bearers of the light of Divine Guidance to the neighbouring countries in that continent, is the object of my fervent prayers at the holy shrines, and the dearest wish of my heart.
>
> *(24 October 1947, LDG Vol. I 129-131)*

| | |
|---|---|
| *Peril* | Danger |
| *Forging* | Moving ahead with effort |
| *Resolved* | Determined in purpose |
| *Consecrated* | Dedicated to a particular purpose |
| *Beset* | Attacked from all sides |
| *Pitfalls* | Potential disasters |
| *Meagre* | Unsatisfactorily small |
| *Propitious* | Favorable and likely to lead to success |
| *Sustain* | Support |

## 72. Reap the Full Harvest

**Construction** began on the superstructure of the Shrine of the Báb in this year, 1949, and in August the second European Teaching Conference was held in Brussels when Shoghi Effendi wrote to the National Spiritual Assembly of Australia and New Zealand:

> ... Obstacles, varied and numerous, will no doubt arise to impede the onward march of this community. Reverses may temporarily dim the radiance of its mission. The forces of religious orthodoxy may well, at a future date, be leagued against it. The exponents of theories and doctrines fundamentally opposed to its religious tenets and social principles may challenge its infant strength with persistence and severity. The Administrative Order - the Ark destined to preserve its integrity and carry it to safety - must without delay, without exception, claim the attention of the members of this community, its ideals must be continually cherished in their hearts, its purposes studied and kept constantly before their eyes, its requirements wholeheartedly met, its laws scrupulously upheld, its institutions unstintingly supported, its glorious mission noised abroad, and its spirit made the sole motivating purpose of their lives.
>
> Then and only then, will this community, so young, so vibrant with life, so rich in promise, so dedicated to its task, be in a position to discharge adequately its weighty responsibilities, to reap the full harvest it has sown, acquire still greater potentialities for the conduct of subsequent stages in the crusade on which it has embarked, and contribute, to a degree unsuspected as yet by its members, its full share to the World-wide establishment of the Faith of Bahá'u'lláh, the emancipation of its Oriental followers, the recognition of its independence, the birth of its World Order and the emergence of that world civilization which that Order is destined to create.

*(22 August 1949, LAN 79-81)*

| | |
|---|---|
| *Impede* | To interfere with the movement, progress or development of something |
| *Leagued* | Joined together |
| *Tenets* | Doctrines or principles |
| *Persistence* | Steadfast holding to a purpose |
| *Scrupulously* | Showing careful regard for what is morally right |
| *Unstintingly* | Generously |

## 73. Carry on the Torch

In the year 1949, construction began on the superstructure of the Shrine of the Báb; the second European Teaching Conference was held in Brussels; and Shoghi Effendi wrote this letter to the National Spiritual Assembly of the British Isles:

> The Bahá'í world, in its entirety, is struck with amazement at the quality of the work performed, at the extent and number of the victories achieved by this community. Its sister-community in the great Republic of the West, already laden with many and splendid trophies gathered in distant fields and over a long period of time cannot regard this resurgence of the Bahá'í spirit, this manifestation of Bahá'í solidarity, these ennobling evidences of Bahá'í achievement, amidst so conservative a people, within so short a time, under such trying circumstances, and by so small a band of workers, except with feelings compounded of envy, of admiration and respect. Its sister-communities throughout the East, venerable by reason of their age, and the sacrifices they have made, and fully aware of the long period of incubation this community has undergone, recall, with feelings of delight, 'Abdu'l-Bahá's prediction, forecasting the germination, at their appointed time, of the potent seeds His loving hands have sown in the course of His twice-repeated visit to that Island, and marvel at the rapidity with which its soil is now manifesting the potentialities with which it has been endowed. He Who blessed it with His footsteps, Who called into being, and fostered the growth of, the community labouring in that Island, hails, from His station on high, the exploits which immortalise the small band of His present-day consecrated and resolute followers, who are carrying on the torch which He Himself had entrusted to their immediate predecessors. Bahá'u'lláh Himself lauds the conspicuous victories being won in His Name, in the dawning years of the Second Bahá'í Century, at the very heart and centre of the greatest Empire the world has ever seen, whose Sovereign Monarch He Himself had addressed and whose deeds He, with His Own pen, had commended.
>
> *(9 April 1949, UD 226-227)*

| | |
|---|---|
| *Resurgence* | The act or process of rising again or becoming stronger again |
| *Compounded* | Mixed; combined to make a whole |
| *Venerable* | Worthy of respect |
| *Incubation* | Gradual development |
| *Germination* | Sprouting and growing |
| *Potent* | Strong, effective and powerful |

| | |
|---|---|
| *Endowed* | Given a quality or ability |
| *Hails* | Praises or approves a person, action or accomplishment |
| *Exploits* | Interesting or daring actions or achievements |
| *Immortalise* | Make someone's memory live on |
| *Consecrated* | Dedicated to a particular purpose |
| *Resolute* | Having determination |
| *Entrusted* | Given somebody responsibility for something |
| *Lauds* | Praises; glorifies |
| *Conspicuous* | Easy to notice; obvious |
| *Commended* | To praise somebody or something in a formal way |

## 74. A Still More Convincing Demonstration of Spirit

In 1956, Shoghi Effendi acquired the title to the Pilgrim House at Bahji from the Israeli government as part of the exchange for the Bahá'í properties at Ein Gev; he also bought the ruined house known as the Master's Tea House. In April he announced that the Bahá'í Faith was established in 247 countries, in 3,700 localities and that there were more than 900 local spiritual assemblies, of which 168 were incorporated; Bahá'í literature had been translated into 190 languages. Three months later he wrote to the National Spiritual Assembly of Germany and Austria:

> The stalwart German Bahá'í Community, ranking among the oldest and certainly one of the most eminent, communities in Europe; firmly implanted in the heart of that continent; constituting one of the leading strongholds of the Faith within its confines; reassured, time and again, through the glowing promises given it, in unmistakable language, by the Centre of the Covenant, in the early years of that community's existence; blessed so abundantly through His memorable visit to its homeland; hardened and chastened in the school of adversity; emerging triumphant over those adversaries that sought so ineffectively to arrest its march, dim its hopes, and disrupt its foundations; fully equipped through more than three decades of Bahá'í administrative experience - such a community finds itself, at this historic hour, fully and hopefully launched upon an enterprise which, if successfully carried out, will enable it to bring to a conclusion a chapter of the utmost significance in the evolution of the Faith of Bahá'u'lláh in that land.
>
> Aware of its manifold responsibilities, determined to fulfill the dearest hopes cherished for it by 'Abdu'l-Bahá, conscious of its inherent strength, and encouraged by its multiple and heartwarming accomplishments, this community, in conjunction with its younger sister, must redouble its efforts to scale loftier heights, to plumb greater depths of dedication, to evince a still nobler heroism, and to heighten, by its accomplishments, and, above all, by a still more convincing demonstration of the spirit animating its members, the feelings of admiration which I myself, as well as the believers in other lands, hold them, in consequence of their mighty endeavours and unforgettable exploits in the service, and for the Cause, of Bahá'u'lláh.
>
> May His Spirit ever shine upon, and warm, their hearts. May His precepts ever guide their footsteps, and may His unfailing grace, vouchsafed from the realms on high, be poured forth upon them in

such abundance as to enable them to achieve, in the years immediately ahead, total and complete victory.

*(21 June 1956, LDG Vol. I 269-270)*

| | |
|---|---|
| *Stalwart* | Sturdy and strong |
| *Eminent* | Superior in position, fame or achievement |
| *Constituting* | Making up the whole or a particular part of something |
| *Strongholds* | Places of strong support for a cause |
| *Confines* | The boundaries or limits restricting something |
| *Abundantly* | Richly; fully |
| *Chastened* | Corrected by punishment or suffering |
| *Emerging* | Starting to appear, arise, occur or develop |
| *Disrupt* | To destroy the order or orderly progression of something |
| *Inherent* | Part of the very nature of something and therefore permanently characteristic of it or necessarily involved in it |
| *Conjunction* | The act of joining or combining two or more things |
| *Plumb* | To examine closely or deeply; probe |
| *Evince* | To show a feeling or quality clearly |
| *Animating* | Giving life to; inspiring to action |
| *Exploits* | Brilliant or heroic achievements |
| *Precepts* | Rules or principles that guide somebody's actions, especially ones that guide moral behavior |
| *Vouchsafed* | Granted as a privilege or special favor |

## 75. A Dedication Reminiscent of the Pledges of the Dawn-Breakers

In April 1957, Shoghi Effendi announced that the Faith had been established in 251 countries, that there were more than a thousand local spiritual assemblies, that Baháʼís lived in more than 4,200 localities, that every territory mentioned in the Tablets of the Divine Plan had been opened to the Faith and that Baháʼí literature had been translated into 230 languages. The Treasury Department of Israel had issued an expropriation order for the remaining property held by Covenant-breakers at Bahjí, mainly the dilapidated building north of the mansion. In the same month he wrote to all Baháʼís:

> I appeal, as I close this review of the superb feats already accomplished, in the course of so many campaigns, by the heroic band of the warriors of Baháʼu'lláh, battling in His Name and by His aid for the purification, the unification and the spiritualization of a morally and spiritually bankrupt society, now hovering on the brink of self-destruction, for a renewed dedication, at this critical hour in the fortunes of mankind, on the part of the entire company of my spiritual brethren in every continent of the globe, to the high ideals of the Cause they have espoused, as well as to the immediate accomplishment of the goals of the Crusade on which they have embarked, be they in active service or not, of either sex, young as well as old, rich or poor, whether veteran or newly enrolled - a dedication reminiscent of the pledges which the Dawn-breakers of an earlier Apostolic Age, assembled in conference at Badasht, and faced with issues of a different but equally challenging nature, willingly and solemnly made for the prosecution of the collective task with which they were confronted.
>
> *(April 1957 MBW 120)*

| | |
|---|---|
| *Feats* | Remarkable acts or achievements involving courage, skill or strength |
| *Espoused* | Adopted or supported something like a belief or cause |
| *Reminiscent* | Suggesting memories of the past |
| *Solemnly* | Deeply and sincerely |
| *Prosecution* | The carrying out of an activity or occupation |

## 76. Not To Be Deflected for a Moment

**In 1957,** one month before Shoghi Effendi wrote this to the National Spiritual Assembly of the Benelux Countries, the Covenant-breakers completely abandoned Bahjí; and two months after he wrote this, he announced 'the complete evacuation of the remnant of Covenant-breakers and the transfer of all their belongings from the precincts of the Most Holy Shrine':

> I fully share the joy and exultation that has filled the hearts of the valiant promoters of the Faith throughout the Benelux countries at this latest and most remarkable evidence of the onward march of their beloved Faith in so important an area of the European continent. This memorable milestone (the historic formation of three new Regional Assemblies for Europe) in the evolution of the institutions of Bahá'u'lláh's embryonic Order, now firmly established in each of the sovereign states of Holland, of Belgium and of Luxembourg, augurs well for its future unfoldment and ultimate fruition in those countries.
>
> The efforts, so nobly exerted in the past by the band of pioneers, resident believers and itinerant teachers in each of these states, must, in consequence of the auspicious opening of a new phase in the establishment of this Divine Order, be multiplied a hundredfold, and the standard of consecration and of service to His Cause must be raised to still greater heights. No obstacle, however formidable, no test or trial however severe, should deflect them for a moment from the task they have pledged themselves to fulfil.
>
> *(5 July 1957, DC 150-151,)*

| | |
|---|---|
| *Exultation* | Extreme happiness or rejoicing |
| *Valiant* | Brave and steadfast |
| *Milestone* | Important event |
| *Embryonic* | Being in the earliest stages of development |
| *Augurs* | Indicates what will happen |
| *Auspicious* | Promising well for future |
| *Consecration* | Dedication |
| *Formidable* | Difficult to deal with or overcome |
| *Severe* | Extremely unpleasant |
| *Deflect* | Cause to turn aside |

Photograph by Nayyirih G. de Koning-Tahzib

# Abbreviations

| | |
|---|---|
| **BA** | Bahá'í Administration |
| **CC** | Compilation of Compilations |
| **CF** | Citadel of Faith |
| **DC** | Dear Co-worker |
| **DND** | Dawn of a New Day |
| **GPB** | God Passes By |
| **HE** | High Endeavors Messages to Alaska |
| **LAN** | Letters from the Guardian to Australia and New Zealand |
| **LDG** | The Light of Divine Guidance |
| **MA** | Messages to **America** Selected Letters and Cablegrams Addressed to the Bahá'ís of North America, 1932-1946 |
| **MBW** | Messages to the Bahá'í World, 1950-1957 |
| **MC** | Messages to Canada |
| **MSI** | Messages of Shoghi Effendi to the Indian Subcontinent |
| **PDC** | The Promised Day is Come |
| **UD** | Unfolding Destiny |
| **WOB** | The World Order of Bahá'u'lláh |

## Bibliography

*A Basic Bahá'í Chronology,* Glenn Cameron with Wendi Momen. George Ronald, Oxford, 1996.
*Bahá'í Administration: Selected Messages, 1922-1932.* Wilmette, Ill.: Bahá'í Publishing Trust, 1968.
*Citadel of Faith: Messages to America, 1947-1957.* Wilmette, Ill.: Bahá'í Publishing Trust, 1965.
*Dawn of a New Day: Messages to India, 1923-1957.* New Delhi: Bahá'í Publishing Trust, undated.
*Dear Co-worker: Messages from Shoghi Effendi to the Benelux countries.* Leuven, Belgium: Brilliant Books, 2009.
*High Endeavors: Messages to Alaska.* National Spiritual Assembly of the Bahá'ís of Alaska, 1976.
*Letters from the Guardian to Australia and New Zealand, 1923-1957.* National Spiritual Assembly of the Bahá'ís of Australia Incorporated, 1971.
*Messages to America: Selected Letters and Cablegrams Addressed to the Bahá'ís of North America, 1932-1946.* Wilmette, Ill.: Bahá'í Publishing Trust, 1947.
*Messages to Canada.* National Spiritual Assembly of the Bahá'ís of Canada, 1965.
*Messages to the Bahá'í World, 1950-1957.* Wilmette, Ill.: Bahá'í Publishing Trust, 1958.
*The Advent of Divine Justice.* Wilmette, Ill.: Bahá'í Publishing Trust, 1963.
*The Light of Divine Guidance: The Messages from the Guardian of the Bahá'í Faith to the Bahá'ís of Germany and Austria.* National Spiritual Assembly of the Bahá'ís of Germany, Bahá'í-Verlag BmbH, 1982.
*The Promised Day is Come.* Wilmette, Ill.: Bahá'í Publishing Trust, 1951.
*The Unfolding Destiny of the British Bahá'í Community: The Messages from the Guardian of the Bahá'í Faith to the Bahá'í Community of the British Isles.* London: Bahá'í Publishing Trust, 1981.
*The World Order of Bahá'u'lláh: Selected Letters.* Wilmette, Ill.: Bahá'í Publishing Trust, 1955.

www.ingramcontent.com/pod-product-compliance
Lightning Source LLC
Chambersburg PA
CBHW020003050426
42450CB00005B/289